To Nick

Only in Canada, You Say

A Treasury of Canadian Language

Katherine Barber

Canada's Word Lady

Enjoy the difference!
We are definately Not American!

OXFORD
UNIVERSITY PRESS

Love,
Jo Anne

OXFORD
UNIVERSITY PRESS

70 Wynford Drive, Don Mills, Ontario M3C 1J9
www.oup.com/ca

Oxford University Press is a department of the University of Oxford.
It furthers the University's objective of excellence in research, scholarship,
and education by publishing worldwide in

Oxford New York

Auckland Cape Town Dar es Salaam Hong Kong Karachi
Kuala Lumpur Madrid Melbourne Mexico City Nairobi
New Delhi Shanghai Taipei Toronto

With offices in

Argentina Austria Brazil Chile Czech Republic France Greece
Guatemala Hungary Italy Japan Poland Portugal Singapore
South Korea Switzerland Thailand Turkey Ukraine Vietnam

Oxford is a trade mark of Oxford University Press
in the UK and in certain other countries

Published in Canada
by Oxford University Press

Library and Archives Canada Cataloguing in Publication

Barber, Katherine, 1959–

Only in Canada, you say : a treasury of Canadian language / Katherine Barber.

Includes index.
ISBN 978-0-19-542984-8

1. Canadianisms (English). 2. English language—Etymology. I. Title.

FC23.B37 2007   427'.971   C2007-900406-7

1 2 3 4 – 11 10 09 08

Cover Illustration: Luc Normandin / Three in a Box

This book is printed on paper which contains 100% post-consumer waste.
Printed in Canada.

CONTENTS

INTRODUCTION

When we set out to prepare the *Canadian Oxford Dictionary* in 1992, we found that Canadians suffered from a profound ignorance about their language. True, most of them knew that our predilection for the tag "eh" was somehow distinctive, as is our pronunciation of the vowel in "out". Some of them perhaps had been stymied in their attempts to order a Caesar in an American bar. And most of them felt quite strongly that "Canadian spelling" consisted of spelling "colour" with an "-our". But alongside this, I had the experience of journalists asking me, "But is there really such a thing as Canadian English? Do we really need a dictionary?", and, perhaps more tellingly, of a casual conversation with someone who opined that if I worked for Oxford University Press, surely I should be interested in "proper English, not Canadian English".

By the time the dictionary came out, in 1998, the same journalists who had been unaware that Canadian English existed were now asking me for "sexy Canadianisms". But in fact what captured people's attention was not the sexy Canadianisms (which were admittedly in short supply), but the ordinary words of our everyday lives that people had not realized were distinctly Canadian: "eavestrough", "Arborite", "Gravol", "butter tart", "joe job". The Canadian public embraced the dictionary enthusiastically, and not just because they wanted to know whether our winter hats are "tuques" or "toques". For the dictionary was tangible proof that Canadians are a distinct people, no longer subjugated (or so we would hope) to the dominant powers of Britain or the United States.

But Canadians kept asking us for a separate list of words that are unique to Canada. *Only in Canada, You Say . . .* is a response to that. It is not a comprehensive "dictionary of Canadianisms". It is meant to be an entertaining, thematically organized list of words unique to or strongly identified with Canadian English. It includes many (but not all) of the Canadianisms in the *Canadian Oxford Dictionary*, and even some which did not meet the rigorous inclusion criteria for that book but have their place here for their entertainment value. It does not include words created by Canadians ("kerosene", "insulin", etc.) or which first entered English on Canadian territory ("kayak", "chipmunk", "toboggan", "McIntosh apple", "lacrosse") if these have gone on to become part of World English. Our selection was based on whether the word reveals something about Canada, when seen with other semantically related words, or whether the word would evoke a "Who knew that was used only in Canada?" reaction. It must be emphasized that in many cases, it is not the *word* so much as a single *meaning* of the word that is unique to Canada. Obviously the word "collector" is not a Canadianism when referring to philatelists, but it is when referring to lanes along an expressway like the 401 in Toronto. Some of the words are trademarks that have come to be used generically in Canada. This phenomenon occurs in all languages. Their inclusion in the book does not imply that they have acquired for legal purposes a non-proprietary or general significance. We are not making any judgment about their legal status.

Some of the words listed here may also be used in US border states or even in parts of other countries ("hydro" to mean electricity, for instance, is also used in Tasmania!) but they are not part of general World English and are perceived by Canadians as central to our identity. Some ("GST", for example, which is also used in New Zealand) have been included simply because their exclusion would seem like an oversight. We have included a separate section of words that Canadian English shares with British English, because Canadians are usually surprised to discover that Americans don't use them.

Word histories have been included only when they are particularly interesting from a Canadian point of view.

For more detailed information about the geographical distribution of a word, its etymology, or grammatical information (spelling variants, irregular plurals, etc.), please consult the *Canadian Oxford Dictionary*.

I hope that *Only in Canada, You Say* . . . will help those from other English-speaking countries to understand Canadians, but that it will also help us to understand—and celebrate—ourselves.

CANADIANS SAY THE DARNEDEST THINGS

Oaths, Imprecations, Epithets, and Insults
🍁 *Fun CanSpeak Facts:* Eh 🍁

Who Knew it was Canadian?

Phrases

Eh

"What about eh?" people invariably ask me when I give talks about Canadian English. Canadians are inordinately proud of this one-sound particle as a marker of Canadian identity. This pride is a little mystifying to me, since there is more—much more—to Canadian English than "eh". When it is used in a phrase like "nice day, eh?", which solicits an affirmative response from the person you're talking to, "eh" is not unique to Canadian English. Americans do not use it, preferring "huh" instead (and yet they do not celebrate "huh" as a marker of their identity). As a result, Americans comment on it as an identifier of Canadians, but English speakers throughout the Commonwealth also use "eh" in this way, as what linguists call a "tag ending".

Where "eh" is uniquely Canadian is in the so-called "narrative eh", for instance in "I'm going to Winnipeg for Christmas, eh, so I'm packing my long johns." The person saying this is not expecting their interlocutor to say "Yes, indeed, you are going to Winnipeg." It is just a filler word, almost as if we want to ascertain that the other person is still listening to us. Other statements, like one I heard my bus driver making, "The bus stalled three times coming down, eh?", are similar. Another classic Canadian use of "eh" is in a phrase that I use myself a lot. Say your neighbour exclaims, "Geez, those dogs barking are driving me crazy"; you might respond, "Really, eh." You are not expecting the neighbour to reply in turn, "Yes, really, you nitwit". You are just making your agreement more emphatic.

The rest of this book should convince you that Canadian English is a vibrant dialect with many words rich in meaning that are unique to us and much more interesting than our tag ending. No kidding, eh.

Oaths and Intensifiers

eh
> *informal* ascertaining the comprehension, continued interest, agreement, etc. of the person or persons addressed .

fuddle duddle
> *euphemism* go to hell; drop dead. ❑ **Origin**: what Prime Minister Pierre Trudeau claimed he said in Parliament rather than a profanity.

holy jumpin'
> *slang* expressing surprise, disbelief, etc. ❑ **Origin**: possibly a corruption of or euphemism for "Holy Jesus".

jeezly
> *slang* damned. ❑ **Origin**: corruption of "Jesus".

skookum
> *(West) informal* excellent, impressive, good. ❑ **Origin**: designating a monster in a Washington Salishan language, then meaning "inspiring fear", becoming "powerful" in Chinook Jargon.

Nicknames Nasty and Nice

Bluenose / Bluenoser

informal a Nova Scotian.

> The origin of this term has been variously explained as referring to fishermen's noses blue from cold, to the name of a potato with a blue protuberance, or to Scots Presbyterians referred to as "true blue" in the 17th century.

cake

derogatory or *jocular* (among Italian-Canadians) a non-Italian white person, especially of British stock, with characteristically North American traits or customs; a mangia-cake.

come from away / CFA

(*Atlantic Canada*) a person who is not from the Atlantic region generally.

dogan

slang offensive a Roman Catholic, especially an Irish Roman Catholic.

herring choker

(*Maritimes*) *informal* a Maritimer, especially a New Brunswicker.

hoser

slang **1** an idiot; a goof. **2** an uncultivated person, especially an unintelligent, inarticulate, beer-drinking lout.

mangia-cake

derogatory or *jocular* (among Italian-Canadians) a non-Italian white person, especially of British stock, with characteristically

North American traits or customs. ❏ **Pronunciation**: "MUNGE a cake". **Origin**: Italian from *mangiare* "eat" + "cake".

pea soup / pea-souper

dated slang offensive a French Canadian.

pepsi

dated informal derogatory a French Canadian. ❏ **Origin**: from the perceived Québécois preference for Pepsi.

sook / sooky baby

(*Atlantic Canada*) *derogatory* a person acting childishly; a wimp, coward, or sissy. ❏ **Pronunciation**: Rhymes with *book*. **Origin**: English dialect "suck", used to call a calf.

suck

1 a crybaby or sore loser; a person who refuses to participate or go along, especially out of spite; a feeble, self-pitying person. **2** a person who behaves obsequiously to those in authority, especially a child.

vendu

derogatory a Québécois who is viewed as having sold out or become assimilated to English-Canadian society.

WHO KNEW IT WAS CANADIAN?

---

aft

informal afternoon.

airtram

(*BC*) an aerial cable car.

animator

a person employed at a historic site to act the part of a typical resident of the time or an actual historical figure associated with the site.

bargoon

slang a bargain.

Block Parent

proprietary one of a number of police-screened volunteers who offer their home, identified by an easily recognizable sign, as an emergency refuge to children or others who are lost or in danger.

bumwad

slang toilet paper.

Cerlox

proprietary a type of reusable plastic binding with teeth that lock into rectangular holes punched in the paper.

eavestrough / eavestroughing

a shallow trough attached to the eaves of a building to collect runoff from the roof; a rain gutter.

EnerGuide

designating a rating of an appliance indicating its typical annual energy consumption.

huck

(*West*) *informal* throw.

rangy
> *informal* restless, uncontrollable, and bad-tempered, especially because of pent-up energy. ❑ **Pronunciation**: "RANG ee".

rubby / rubbydub
> *slang* a person who drinks rubbing alcohol, aftershave, etc. mixed with cheap wine etc.; a derelict alcoholic.

schmuck
> *slang* hit, flatten.

shit disturber
> *slang* a person who enjoys causing trouble or discord.

spinny
> *slang* crazy, foolish.

stickhandle
> manoeuvre (a project etc.) skilfully through obstacles.

stunned
> *informal* stupid; foolish.

sucky
> *slang* whiny, like a crybaby.

wingy
> *informal* crazy, flighty, loopy.

PHRASES

have had the biscuit
be no longer good for anything; be done for.

cheap like borscht
extremely cheap.

a pinch of coonshit
coarse slang a negligible or contemptible quantity.

done like dinner
utterly defeated.

dream in Technicolor
be wildly unrealistic.

it'll be a frosty Friday (in July)
it is unlikely to happen.

give someone the gears
pester, hassle.

take off the gloves
ready oneself or indicate readiness for a confrontation.

no guff
1 a declaration of truthfulness. **2** an expression of mock surprise at a statement.

hang up one's skates
give up; quit or retire.

kick at the can

an opportunity to do something.

rag the puck

waste time intentionally.

rhyme off

recite rapidly and spontaneously (a list of items).

saw off

compromise by trading concessions.

go snaky

lose self-control.

stoop and scoop

pick up the excrement of one's pet in public places.

make strange

(of a baby or child) fuss or be shy in company.

go to the washroom

defecate or urinate.

as well

furthermore, moreover.

  Canadians seem more likely than other English speakers to use "as well" at the beginning of a sentence, as in *As well, Albertans are very friendly.*

A COUNTRY WITH TOO MUCH GEOGRAPHY

Land of Snow and Ice

✤ Fun CanSpeak Facts: The Great White North ✤

Weather

Water, Water, Everywhere

Life in the Great Outdoors

The Great White North

Canadians use many words in reference to the winter, a lot of them unprintable, but there is no escaping that in those parts of the country outside what we like to call "Lotusland" in southern BC, the winter has had a formative effect on our language.

Transportation in winter has always presented Canadians with a particular challenge; one solution to the problem is the ingenious winter road, a road made of compacted snow or ice often plowed over a frozen lake or muskeg or other ground that could not support a road in summer. Winter roads, which are mentioned as early as 1800 in Canadian sources, are still a very important link in the transportation system of northern Canada. People tell hair-raising stories about being halfway across a lake on a winter road and seeing a huge crack opening up in the middle of the road, threatening to swallow their truck.

Another form of winter-only road is the ice bridge. This phenomenon happens when a river freezes over solidly enough for people and vehicles to pass over it. Many places that have ferries in summer have ice bridges in the winter.

If you're winter camping or if you get stuck out in the snow, you will be very grateful to know about an invention of Canada's northern Aboriginal peoples, the quinzhee. This snow shelter is created by piling up snow, letting it settle, then hollowing out the interior. It comes from an Athapaskan word meaning "bowl-shaped depression in the snow".

Back in the city, winter can cause us some major problems, and has resulted in some uniquely Canadian uses of words. Take the word "windrow" for example. In most varieties of English, this is an agricultural term, meaning a line of raked hay or sheaves laid out for drying by the wind. Canadians know it as that annoying heap of snow left by the passage of a snowplow—usually right across the end of your driveway just after you've finished shovelling it! You may also have a less polite name for it.

Perhaps a solution would be to recruit a caribou instead of your trusty snowblower to remove snow. The word "caribou" literally means "snow shoveller". It comes to us from Mi'kmaq via French; the animal was called this by the Mi'kmaq because of its habit of scooping away the snow to get at the food lying under it.

But winter isn't all shovelling and shivering. Canadians have become past masters at enjoying the winter, even inventing sports such as barrel-jumping to while away the time. We've got to do something to keep ourselves going till "breakup", a word that we use to designate the thawing of the rivers and lakes in the spring. English-speakers from other countries use "breakup" only in the political sense ("the breakup of the Soviet Union") and the romantic sense ("she's going through a really bad breakup"). What must they think when they hear Canadians talking about "spring breakup"? That we dump our significant others every year and start over?

Come with us on a trip through the vocabulary of the Great White North.

'Twas in the Moon of Wintertime

freeze-up

the freezing up of a river, lake, etc., especially in the fall.

nordicity

a measure of the degree of northernness of a high-latitude place, calculated by assigning values to ten criteria, including latitude, summer heat, and annual cold.

Plus-15

(in Calgary) an enclosed overhead walkway between buildings.

(spring) breakup

1 the breaking of a frozen river etc. into blocks of ice at the spring thaw. **2** the time during which this happens.

storm-stayed

(*Maritimes* & *Southwestern Ontario*) stranded due to severe or inclement weather conditions; snowbound.

windrow

a ridge of snow, gravel, etc. heaped along the side of a road by a snowplow, grader, etc.

winter club

an organization that offers access to various recreational facilities for activities such as skating and curling throughout the winter.

How many different words for ice?

ballicatter

(*Newfoundland*) ice formed along a shoreline from waves and freezing spray. Pronounced "bala KATTER". ❑ **Origin**: alteration of "barricade".

bay ice

(*Newfoundland*) ice formed in a single winter on the surface of a bay or harbour.

blue ice

a vivid blue ice formed when a large amount of water freezes quickly.

candle

(of ice) deteriorate into candle-like icicles.

candle ice

ice which has deteriorated into candle-like icicles before breaking up.

clumper / clumpet

(*Atlantic Canada*) a large floating chunk of ice.

frazil

slush consisting of small ice crystals formed in water too turbulent to freeze over. ❑ **Origin**: Canadian French *frasil* "snow floating in the water"; compare French *fraisil* "cinders".

glib ice

(especially *PEI*) ice that is slippery, smooth.

glitter

(*Newfoundland*) **1** freezing rain. **2** the coating of ice deposited by a glitter storm.

ice candle

(*Newfoundland*) an icicle.

ice pan

a slab of floating ice.

lolly

(*Atlantic Canada*) slush consisting of small ice crystals formed in water too turbulent to freeze over; frazil. ❑ **Origin**: British dialect "loblolly" = "thick soup or porridge".

rotten

designating ice or snow which, in the course of melting, has become granular and weak; disintegrating.

rough ice

a large bank of ice that has accumulated on the shore of a river from the freezing of successive tides.

running ice

(*Atlantic Canada*) ice that is moving, carried by currents or the wind.

silver thaw

(*Atlantic Canada*) a slick glassy coating of ice formed on the ground or an exposed surface, caused by freezing rain or a sudden light frost.

slob (ice)

sludgy masses of densely packed sea ice.

North of 60

agloo / aglu

a breathing hole made by a seal through sea ice.

angakok

an Inuit shaman or healer. ❏ **Pronunciation**: "ANG uh coke".

babiche

strips of rawhide or sinew used as laces, thread, webbing, etc., e.g. in snowshoes. ❏ **Origin**: Canadian French from Mi'kmaq.

bearpaw snowshoe

an almost circular, tailless type of snowshoe.

fan hitch

a method of harnessing sled dogs, with the lead dog on a long trace and the other dogs arranged in a fan-shaped pattern on either side.

inukshuk / inuksuk

a figure of a human made of stones, originally used among the Inuit to scare caribou into an ambush, and as a marker to guide travellers, now also found as decorative sculptures in southern Canada. ❏ **Pronunciation**: "in NOOK shook".

komatik / qamutik

an Inuit sled consisting of two parallel wooden runners connected by wooden slats, usually pulled by a dog team or snowmobile. ❏ **Pronunciation**: "COMMA tick".

Qallunaaq / Kabloona

(*North*) a person who is not Inuit, especially a white person.
❏ **Pronunciation**: "kuh LOON ack" / "kuh BLUE nuh". **Origin**:
Inuktitut, literally "people with the bushy eyebrows".

qiviut

fine, soft wool from the underbelly of a muskox. ❏ **Pronunciation**: "KIVVY oot".

qulliq / kudlik

an Inuit soapstone seal oil lamp, providing both light and heat.
❏ **Pronunciation**: "CULL lick" / "KUDE lick".

shiptime

historical the annual arrival of a supply ship in the North after
the ice breaks up.

stroud

a coarse woollen cloth used especially in the North to make
blankets, leggings, etc. ❏ **Origin**: perhaps from the town of
Stroud in Gloucestershire, England, known for its woollen
mills.

tupik

a traditional skin tent used by Inuit groups during the summer.

ulu

an Inuit knife consisting of a semicircular or crescent-shaped
blade and a handle centred behind the non-cutting edge, traditionally used by women.

utilidor

(*North*) an enclosed insulated conduit running above ground and carrying water, sewerage, and electricity between houses in settlements built on permafrost. Pronounced "you TILLA dore". ❑ **Origin**: blend of "utility" + "corridor".

WEATHER

---

chinook arch

a bow-shaped cloud formation bordering an expanse of clear sky, visible on the western Prairies before or during a chinook wind.

great white combine

(*Saskatchewan*) *slang* hail.

humidex

a scale indicating the personal discomfort level resulting from combined heat and humidity, calculated by adding a given value based on the dew point level to the temperature of the atmosphere. ❑ **Origin**: blend of "humidity" + "index", first used by the Toronto Weather Office in 1965.

streamer

an elongated band of clouds, ranging from 10 to 20 km in width and from 50 to 100 km in length, formed by convection around the Great Lakes, and generating large amounts of localized snow.

suete

(*Cape Breton*) a very strong southeasterly wind in the west coastal areas of the Cape Breton Highlands. Pronounced "swet". ❏ **Origin**: Acadian French, corruption of French *sud-est* "southeast".

wreckhouse winds

extremely strong winds which blow across Cape Ray from the Long Range Mountains in Newfoundland.

WATER, WATER, EVERYWHERE

---

angle

(*Newfoundland*) a curved inlet in a lake or pond.

back bay

a shallow bay off a lake.

back channel

a backwater or side channel of a river.

back eddy

(especially *BC*) an area of water behind an obstruction in a watercourse in which the current is the reverse of the general direction of flow.

barachois / barrasway

(*Atlantic Canada*) a shallow coastal lagoon or pond created by the formation of a sandbar a short distance offshore from a beach.

barren

(*New Brunswick & Nova Scotia*) an expanse of marsh or muskeg.

chute

a rapid on a river.

government wharf

a public wharf built and maintained by the government.

headpond

(*Maritimes*) a pond created behind a dam.

height of land

a watershed.

lakehead

the area along a lakeshore farthest from the lake's outlet.

overflow

an overflow of water from beneath the frozen surface of a river, lake, etc.

rattle

(*Newfoundland & Nova Scotia*) rapids or fast-flowing water.

reversing falls

a set of rapids on a tidal river, the flow of which reverses regularly due to the pressure of the incoming tide.

side channel

a shallow and narrow tributary running into a river.

slough

1 (*BC*) a shallow inlet or estuary lined with grass. **2** (*Prairies*) a small marshy pool or lake produced by rain or melting snow flooding a depression in the soil.

Western Canadians may be surprised to discover that a ubiquitous feature of the prairie landscape, the slough, which for them rhymes with "who", is pronounced by most other English speakers to rhyme with "how". The word can be traced back to before 900 AD. It seems that throughout the Middle Ages there were various pronunciations of the word. "Slew" may have been a more northern or Scottish pronunciation; for instance, the word "plough" was pronounced "ploo" in Scottish English. It would make sense for a Scottish pronunciation to become prevalent in the Prairies, since the Scottish Selkirk Settlers were the first English-speaking permanent residents of the West.

snye

(*Eastern Ontario*) a side channel, especially one that bypasses a falls or rapids and rejoins the main river downstream, creating an island. ❑ **Origin**: Canadian French *chenail*, French *chenal* "channel".

steady

(*Newfoundland*) **1** a stretch of still water in a river or pond; a pool. **2** a small freshwater pond.

swift

an area of rapidly flowing current in a river.

tickle

(*Atlantic Canada*) **1** a narrow strait or channel between islands or between an island and the mainland, especially one that is difficult to navigate. **2** an entrance to a harbour that is narrow and difficult to navigate.

Parks

ecogift
a donation to the federal, provincial, or municipal government, or to a charitable organization, of land or of an interest in land that has been designated as environmentally sensitive, e.g. wetlands, forests, grasslands, etc.

monkey trail
(*West*) a narrow trail, in a park, field, along a riverbank, etc. created by the passage of walkers, cyclists, etc.

parkette
(*Southern Ontario*) a small park in a city, usually less than a block and containing a grassy area, small gardens, benches, etc.

Camping and Hiking

featherstick
a stick of wood of which one end is cut into thin strips in a fan shape, to make more effective kindling.

lobstick
a tall, conspicuous coniferous tree that has had all but its uppermost branches lopped off, serving as a landmark, a monument, or a talisman.

mug-up

a break for a hot drink (especially tea) and snacks, especially while on a hike, journey, etc.

outpost camp

a remote hunting or fishing camp.

SAR Tech

a search and rescue technician, a non-commissioned member of the Canadian Forces specialized in performing rescue operations at crash and emergency sites, and highly trained in such related skills as parachuting, mountain climbing, first aid, etc.

signal fire

a small fire or the remnant smoke of an extinguished fire serving to inform others of one's presence at a campsite.

tent ring

a ring of stones for holding down a tent, teepee, etc., especially as encountered indicating a past campsite.

unserviced

(especially of a campsite) not serviced with electricity etc.

Farming

agricultural representative / ag rep

an employee of an agriculture ministry who advises farmers in a particular region.

agri-food

(of an industry) concerned with or involved in the production or processing of food.

agro

(*Saskatchewan*) *informal* a student of agricultural science.

agrologist

a specialist in agricultural science.

agrology

the application of science to agriculture.

back concession

(*Ontario & Quebec*) a concession at some distance from a more heavily settled road or area.

back concessions

(*Ontario & Quebec*) a rural area, especially viewed as conservative or unsophisticated; the boonies.

concession

(*Ontario & Quebec*) a tract of surveyed farmland, itself further divided into lots.

country elevator

(*Prairies*) a grain elevator equipped to unload grain from trucks, store it, and load it into rail cars.

drive shed / driving shed

(especially *Ontario*) a large shed used for storing farm machinery, vehicles, etc.

dugout

(*Prairies*) a large hole, either shallow or with steep sides, used as a reservoir to catch and hold rain, spring runoff, etc.

experimental farm / experimental station

an agricultural research centre, especially one established by the federal government.

First Meridian

the north-south line, 97 degrees 27 minutes west, from which land in the prairies is surveyed.

foodland

farmland; land that is or may be used for the production of food.

horse bun

slang a piece of horse manure.

long lot

a long narrow farm lot extending back from a river, especially one along the St. Lawrence River or in the Red River Settlement.

machine shed

(*West*) a small, auxiliary structure or outbuilding in which machines, equipment, implements, etc. are kept.

Marquis wheat

a variety of wheat which ripens in a relatively short growing season, allowing wheat to be grown further north in Canada.
❑ **Pronunciation**: "MAR kwiss". **Origin**: possibly in honour

of the Marquess of Dufferin and Ava, Governor General of Canada 1872–8.

mussel mud

(*Maritimes*) thick sea mud, rich in lime from the remains of mussels etc., used as fertilizer.

permit book

a document issued annually by the Canadian Wheat Board to a farmer to record deliveries of and payments for the farmer's wheat and barley.

pool

a grain farmers' co-operative for marketing etc.

purple gas

(*Prairies*) gas sold with reduced taxes to farmers for farm machinery and vehicles, dyed purple for identification.

quota

authorization to produce a specified quantity of an agricultural product granted by a marketing board to a farmer.

rang

(*Quebec*) a row of long lots, usually along a road. ❑ **Origin**: French, = "row, range".

Red Fife

a high-yielding variety of wheat, with superior milling and baking qualities, developed in the 1840s near Peterborough, Ontario. ❑ **Origin**: David Fife, Canadian farmer and wheat breeder, d.1877.

shaganappi

(*West*) **1** thread, cord, or thong made of rawhide. **2** a rough pony.

In Swampy Cree, *pishagan* means "leather" and *a-piy* means "string" or "cord". Obviously shaganappi was a staple of life in the Prairies, since it was adaptable to a number of uses, rather like binder twine; in fact, we have one 1873 quotation saying "shaganappi, in this part of the world, does all that leather, cloth, rope, nails, glue, straps, cord, tape .. [the list goes on] are used for elsewhere". Obviously the duct tape of the 1870s! Because many repairs made with shaganappi (like repairs made with binder twine or duct tape) were of an improvised, jury-rigged nature, the word also came to mean "hastily done, of inferior quality", etc. It came to be applied to horses, especially run-down nags, either because of the use of shaganappi in harnesses or as an extension of the "inferior" sense.

stubble-jumper

slang a prairie farmer.

summerfallow

agricultural land left fallow in the summer to allow moisture and nutrient levels to recover.

Texas gate

(*West*) a ditch covered by metal bars spaced so as to allow vehicles and pedestrians to pass over but not cattle or other animals.

trash cover

crop residue left on top of the soil to prevent erosion and moisture loss.

Wheat Board

a Crown corporation responsible for the sale of all wheat and barley produced in Western Canada and destined for export or domestic human consumption.

wheat pool

a grain farmers' co-operative in Western Canada for the sale of wheat and other cereal crops.

Forestry

annual allowable cut

(*BC*) the volume of wood which may be cut each year in a specified area.

barber chair

a tree stump with a large splintered point of wood left above the undercut as a result of improper sawing.

beachcomber

(*BC*) a person who earns a living by collecting logs that have broken loose from log booms and returning them to logging companies.

beehive burner

(*BC*) a dome-shaped incinerator used to burn waste at a sawmill.

berth

a specified area of timberland in which a company or individual is entitled to fell trees.

boom chain

a chain linking two boomsticks, used to hold booms of logs together.

booming ground

a section of a lake, river, etc. where logs are collected into booms.

bush camp

1 the living quarters, offices, etc., of a mining or lumbering operation in the bush. **2** a camp set up for living in the bush.

bushed

1 *informal* (of a person) living in the bush. **2** crazy; insane (due to isolation).

bush fever

any of various physical or emotional disorders caused by protracted isolation in the bush.

bushworker

a logger; a person who works in the bush.

camboose

a large wooden cabin with a central fireplace, serving as a winter shelter in a logging camp.

chicot

a dead tree or dead part of a tree. ❑ **Pronunciation**: "she CO". **Origin**: French, = "stump".

cutline

a line cut through the bush, e.g. as a survey line.

float camp

(*BC*) a log raft supporting the living quarters etc. of a coastal logging crew.

landing

an area where logs are piled before being loaded for transportation.

limit

an area of forested land in which an individual or company has the right to fell and remove timber.

log chute

a chute constructed to allow logs being driven down a river to bypass a waterfall or rapids.

log drive

the transporting of logs from the bush to the mills by floating them down rivers etc.

pike pole

a long pole with a sharp point and hook, used for moving floating logs.

river drive

a log drive down a river.

shanty

historical a logging camp. ❑ **Origin**: perhaps from Canadian French *chantier* "a lumberjack's cabin or logging camp".

shantyman

historical a lumberjack; a worker at a lumber camp.

show

a logging operation.

spar tree

a tree or other tall structure to which cables are attached for hauling logs.

swamper

a person who clears logging roads by felling trees, removing undergrowth, etc.

timber licence

a licence to cut timber from a berth conditional upon payment of dues to the government.

timber rights

the rights to cut timber of a certain diameter in a specified region, which are controlled by the provincial government and may be obtained in exchange for payment.

whistlepunk

(*BC*) *dated* a member of a logging crew who relays to the donkeyman the hooktender's signal that the logs have been secured with chokers and may be hauled away.

Fishing

banking

(*Newfoundland*) fishing for cod off the southeast coast of Newfoundland.

cannonball

(*BC*) a cannonball-like weight tied to commercial fishing lines to control depth and angle.

cod trap

a device used for inshore fishing, consisting of a long net along which fish are guided into a box-shaped trap.

doryman

a person who fishes from a dory.

fishway

a lock built to aid fish in passing a waterfall etc. on their way
upstream to spawn.

herring scull / herring school

(*Newfoundland*) a school of herring appearing in inshore waters.

herring skiff

(*BC*) a broad, flat-bottomed, open, usually aluminum boat with
a low freeboard, used for herring fishing.

ice hole

a hole cut through the ice on the surface of a lake etc., used
for ice fishing.

kakivak

a three-pronged fish spear used by the Inuit.

midshore

designating the fishery an intermediate distance from shore,
between the inshore and the offshore fisheries.

nose

the northeast portion of the Grand Banks of Newfoundland,
lying outside Canada's 320-km (200-mile) fishing zone.

opening

a period of fixed length determined by the government during
which fishing of a specified species (e.g. herring, salmon) may
be undertaken.

outport

1 (*Newfoundland*) any port other than St. John's, especially a small, isolated fishing village. 2 (*Maritimes*) a coastal fishing village.

tail

the southeast portion of the Grand Banks of Newfoundland, lying outside Canada's 320-km (200-mile) fishing zone.

LAND OF THE SILVER BIRCH, HOME OF THE BEAVER

Mammals
🍁 *Fun CanSpeak Facts:* Wile E. Togony 🍁

Fish and Molluscs

Birds

Monsters and Spirits

Plants

Trees

Wile E. Togony

The topic of fauna and flora gives us an opportunity to examine a remarkable quirk of Canadians when it comes to spelling and pronunciation variants: each Canadian believes that his or her linguistic practice is the "true Canadian" one and anything else must be wrong—and probably American to boot. So I have had people who pronounce "missile" to rhyme with "missal" tell me, outraged, that those other Canadians who rhyme it with "mile" are obviously wrong and have sold out to those nefarious Americans. Of course, the truth is that "missal" is the only pronunciation used by Americans, whereas the other pronunciation is used by the British. But Canadians don't usually like to let the truth interfere with a little zealous anti-Americanism.

A flurry of controversy which arose in Toronto a while ago about how to pronounce the word "coyote", prompted by sightings of the animal in an urban park, is a classic example of this, with the added fillip of a dash of Western anti-Ontarianism. Torontonians, whose only previous acquaintance with the animal was seeing it flattened by a cartoon anvil, not surprisingly call it a "ky OAT ee". Westerners, who have lived with the animal longer and traditionally have more commonly said "KY oat" or even "KY oot", may be prompted to launch into a spate of righteous indignation about Ontarians' supposed ignorance, and, worse, their supposed susceptibility to American influences, whereas Westerners are much more impervious to this and can keep true Canadianness alive.

Being a Westerner myself, I too say "KY oat", but I like to take a more dispassionate view. Perhaps we should look into the facts of the case. Just who does say "KY oat" and who does say "ky OAT ee"? Is "KY oat" more "truly Canadian" than "ky OAT ee"? (One of my colleagues at the *Canadian Oxford Dictionary* admitted to me that he had always thought that "KY oat" was the "weird pronunciation", and probably American).

The animal's name is ultimately derived from Nahuatl, the language spoken by the Aztecs, for whom the crafty canine was a "coyotl". Reviving this version of the word might solve all our problems. The fact that it no longer exists can be blamed on the Spanish speakers of Mexico, who were totally unable to pronounce the string "tl" at the end of a word and thus transformed it into the three-syllable "coyote", which is what the English speakers in the Southwestern United States borrowed from them in the early 1800s. It is unclear how the two-syllable variant arose from this, but it is analogous to what happened to the word "chocolate" as it passed into English from the Nahuatl "chocolatl" via Spanish "chocolate". The fact is that for "coyote" all American dictionaries give both pronunciations, some of them with the "KY oat" version first.

Dear God, this means that *both* pronunciations are American!! Now what do we do if we want to be "truly Canadian"? Well, of course they're both American. Where else would we get a Mexican Spanish word for a native animal from? It's hardly likely to have come into Canadian English via Britain, or to have leapfrogged right over the US to land in Canada untarnished. We could of course also ask the philosophical question as to why it would be better if it *had* come from Britain, but the point is moot.

Now, the coyote does go by other names, such as "prairie wolf" or "brush wolf", which would avoid the pronunciation problem but incur the wrath of zoologists who would point out that it is not a wolf. Perhaps a more uniquely Canadian solution would be to revive the words "mishagunis" and "togony" adapted by English speakers such as the explorer John Palliser from Algonquian names for the animal in the 1800s. Good luck if you wish to try this.

It is hardly the environmentally correct thing to suggest that we might enlist the services of a handy roadrunner to ensure that all of Toronto's coyotes are hoist with their own petard (produced by the Acme Petard Company, it goes without saying) and thus spare us the necessity of talking about them at all.

So perhaps we should take the tolerant Canadian view and say "You say KYoat and I say ky OAT ee; let's call the whole thing . . . legitimate pronunciation variation". Try setting that to a Broadway tune!

bell
the dangling appendage under a moose's neck.

Canadian horse
a sturdy black draft horse of a breed developed in Canada by early French settlers.

kermode (bear)
a subspecies of the black bear which can have either black or white fur, found in the coastal mainland and some coastal islands of British Columbia. Pronounced "ker MOE dee".
❑ **Origin**: named for Francis Kermode, director of the Royal British Columbia Museum, d.1946.

Newfoundland pony

a breed of pony found in Newfoundland that has adapted to conditions there by developing a thick winter coat and powerful teeth to eat coarse grasses and shrubs.

Nova Scotia duck tolling retriever

a reddish dog of a breed created by crossing black Labradors with red cocker spaniels, trained to attract ducks along a shoreline and then retrieve them. ❑ **Origin**: from "toll" = "lure or decoy".

silvertip

(*West*) a mature grizzly bear with white-tipped hairs, especially one native to the Rocky Mountains.

spirit bear

a white kermode bear.

FISH AND MOLLUSCS

barbotte / barbot

(*Quebec & Ontario*) the channel catfish, the largest catfish in Canada and an excellent food fish.

bar clam

(*PEI*) a large clam with a corrugated shell, found on underwater sandbars.

Boston bluefish

the pollock, a greenish food fish of the cod family inhabiting the north Atlantic.

capelin / caplin

a small smelt-like fish of the north Atlantic, used as food and as bait for catching cod etc.

Caraquet

a small variety of edible oyster found in the waters off New Brunswick. Pronounced "CAR uh ket". ❏ **Origin**: named after the town of Caraquet, New Brunswick.

conner / connor

(*Newfoundland*) a saltwater bottom-feeding fish, found commonly around rocks and wharves.

doré

the yellow walleye, a major commercial and sport fish. ❏ **Pronunciation**: "door RAY". **Origin**: French, = "golden".

gaspereau

a fish of the herring family, found off the Atlantic coast of North America and in the Great Lakes; an alewife. ❏ **Origin**: Canadian French *gaspareau*.

inconnu / cony

(*North*) a predatory freshwater salmonid game fish of the Eurasian and North American Arctic, important as a food fish in northern Canada. ❏ **Origin**: Canadian French, literally "unknown", because the fish was unfamiliar.

Kamloops trout

a bright silvery rainbow trout found in lakes.

kiack

(*Nova Scotia*) a fish of the herring family found off the Atlantic coast of North America and in the Great Lakes; an alewife. ❏ **Pronunciation**: "KIE ack". **Origin**: probably from Mi'kmaq.

loche

(*North*) a freshwater fish of the cod family, with a broad head and barbels. ❏ **Pronunciation**: "LOSH". **Origin**: French from Old French, from Gaulish *leuka* "whiteness".

Malpeque oyster

a large edible oyster raised in Malpeque Bay, PEI.

mudcat

a North American freshwater catfish having a large head with several barbels.

mud trout

(*Newfoundland*) the eastern brook trout, a popular game fish in eastern Canada.

ouananiche

a landlocked lake variety of Atlantic salmon, found in Newfoundland and Labrador, Quebec, and Ontario. ❏ **Pronunciation**: "WANNA nish". **Origin**: Canadian French from Montagnais *wananish* "little salmon".

Restigouche salmon

a variety of Atlantic salmon associated with the Restigouche River.

spring salmon

a chinook salmon, a large silver-coloured salmon with black spots, native to the north Pacific and introduced into the Great Lakes and elsewhere.

tyee

(*BC*) a chinook salmon, especially one weighing more than 13.6 kg (30 lb.). ❑ **Origin**: Chinook Jargon, from Nuu-chah-nulth *ta:yi:* "elder brother, chief".

Winnipeg goldeye

a silvery freshwater fish with a golden iris, of central North America, much favoured as a delicacy in Manitoba, especially when smoked, when it becomes a reddish-gold colour.

BIRDS

baccalieu bird

(*Newfoundland*) any of various seabirds, especially the Atlantic common murre or the Atlantic common puffin. ❑ **Pronunciation**: "backa LOO". **Origin**: ultimately from Spanish *baccallao* "codfish", believed by early navigators to be the native name in Newfoundland for cod.

bull bird

(*Newfoundland*) the dovekie, a small arctic sea diver with a short stubby bill and a short thick neck.

lords and ladies

the harlequin duck.

noddy

(*Newfoundland*) the Atlantic fulmar, a gull-like bird common in eastern Canadian waters.

ticklace / tickleass

(*Newfoundland*) either of two small gulls, the black-legged kittiwake or the red-legged kittiwake, nesting on sea cliffs.
❏ **Pronunciation:** "TICKLE ass". **Origin**: imitative of its cry.

turr

(*Newfoundland*) an auk or guillemot.

whisky jack

a grey jay, a common North American jay with grey, black, and white plumage, notorious for its boldness in scavenging from backwoods camps and picnic grounds.

Although also known picturesquely as the "camp robber" for its food-filching habits, the "whisky jack" does not usually fly off with a mickey of rye in its beak. Its name has its origins in Cree or Montagnais, both Algonquian languages. In those languages, the name of this bird is *wiskatjan*. *Wiskatjan* also meant "blacksmith", and apparently the bird was called this because of its sooty grey and black plumage. The English newcomers (most likely the employees of the Hudson's Bay Company) in the 18th century assimilated this Cree word into English, heard *wiskatjan* and called it "whisky John". It was a short step to make it more familiar, by using the nickname "Jack" for "John", so "whisky John" ended up as "whisky jack".

MONSTERS AND SPIRITS

bibe

(*Newfoundland*) a creature said to cry at night as an omen of someone's death. ❏ **Origin**: Irish *badhbh* "female fairy or phantom".

Cadborosaurus

a large serpentine sea creature supposedly inhabiting the waters off Victoria, BC. ❏ **Origin**: Cadboro Bay (a bay in Victoria, BC) + Greek *sauros* "lizard".

Ogopogo

an aquatic monster alleged to live in Okanagan Lake, BC. ❏ **Origin**: said to be from a British music hall song.

sasquatch

a supposed manlike furry animal of northwestern North America. ❏ **Origin**: Halkomelem "wild man".

skookum

(*West*) (especially among Aboriginal peoples of the Northwest coast) an evil spirit. ❏ **Origin**: Chinook Jargon "ghost, monster".

Windigo

(in the folklore of Northern Algonquian peoples) a cannibalistic giant; a person who has been transformed into a monster by the consumption of human flesh. ❏ **Origin**: from Ojibwa *wintiko*.

PLANTS

beaver root

(*Newfoundland*) any of several varieties of water lily, especially the fragrant water lily.

prairie crocus

a spring-flowering plant of the buttercup family, found from BC to Manitoba and the US, and covered with silky hairs and with purple or white flowers and long plumed seeds. Floral emblem of Manitoba.

prairie smoke

either of two plants with long-plumed seeds: the purple or three-flowered avens or the prairie crocus.

prairie wool

the natural grassy plant cover of prairie land.

TREES

Acadian forest

the type of forest, characterized by red spruce, balsam fir, yellow birch, and sugar maple, found in Nova Scotia, PEI, and part of New Brunswick.

bluff

(*Prairies*) a grove or clump of trees, usually poplars or willows.

Manitoba maple / bastard maple

a fast-growing North American maple found east of the Rockies.

tuckamore

(*Newfoundland*) **1** a stunted tree or bush, especially a spruce or juniper, with creeping roots and interlacing branches. **2** dense scrub formed by such trees or bushes. ❑ **Origin**: obsolete sense of "tuck" = "tug" + Middle English *more* "tree root".

wolf willow

a silvery-leaved North American oleaster.

GETTING AROUND

The Song My Paddle (or Outboard) Sings
❧ *Fun CanSpeak Facts:* Paddle Your Own ❧

Planes, Trains, and Automobiles

Goin' Down the Road

THE SONG MY PADDLE (OR OUTBOARD) SINGS

Paddle Your Own

In a country whose motto is "From Sea to Sea", we have many boats, but the quintessential Canadian watercraft is the canoe (ironically the word itself is not of Canadian origin: it derives from an aboriginal language of the Caribbean). It's probably safe to say that our country wouldn't exist without canoes, so it's not surprising that we have many different names for them.

My favourite is the bastard canoe of the fur trade, so called because it was halfway between the biggest canoe and the smallest and could be used on lakes or rivers, but no doubt a very useful epithet when the voyageurs were lugging the two tons of freight it contained over a portage. Not the type of canoe you'd need if you had to get something to someone in a hurry.

For that, there were "express canoes", the Purolator of the fur trade. But "express" certainly didn't mean overnight delivery: it took over a month to paddle from Montreal to the Lakehead. Then again, life was at a slower pace: Jean-Baptiste Lagimodière, travelling flat out (much of it by snowshoe), took five months to take "urgent" dispatches from the Red River Colony in 1815 to Lord Selkirk in Montreal. If only he'd had email!

"A Canadian," Pierre Berton famously said, "is someone who knows how to make love in a canoe." Here we offer you a selection, should you wish to demonstrate the truth of that dictum.

Canoes

bastard canoe / batard

a birchbark canoe used in the fur trade, about 9 m (30 ft.) long and capable of carrying about 2000 kg (two tons) of freight.
❑ **Origin**: Canadian French *canot bâtard*.

canot du maître / Montreal canoe

the largest birchbark canoe of the fur trade, up to 12 m (40 ft.) long, used between the St. Lawrence River and Lake Superior.
❑ **Pronunciation**: "can oh doo METTRA". **Origin**: French, = "canoe of the master".

cedarstrip

a technique for making boats, especially canoes, consisting of long strips of cedar.

express canoe

a relatively small, light canoe of the fur trade, usually lightly burdened to increase speed of important deliveries.

freight canoe

a large canoe of the fur trade used for transporting freight.

Gander Bay boat

(*Newfoundland*) a large canoe-like boat used on the lower stretches of the Gander River.

ice canoe

a small, sturdy boat used to cross a partially frozen river.

Peterborough canoe

a type of all-wood canoe originally built at Peterborough, Ontario.

rabaska

(*Quebec*) a large birchbark or cedar canoe, about 8 m long with a high, usually decorated, bow and stern, which can hold 10 to 12 people. ❏ **Origin**: Canadian French, alteration of "Athabaska", the canoes being originally used for the fur trade into the Athabaska region.

voyageur canoe / canot du nord / north canoe

a birchbark canoe of the fur trade, about 9 m (30 ft.) long, used on the rivers and lakes northwest of Lake Superior.

Other Watercraft

banker

1 a fishing boat operating in the waters off Newfoundland, especially the Grand Banks. **2** a Newfoundland fisherman.

bateau

a light, shallow-draft, flat-bottomed boat with pointed bow and stern, especially of the kind used by fur traders, propelled by oars, poles, or sails, or drawn by horses. ❏ **Origin**: French, = "boat".

bay boat

(*Newfoundland*) a boat that carries passengers, mail, and supplies to coastal areas of Newfoundland.

bully (boat)

(*Newfoundland*) a two-masted decked boat used for fishing on the coasts of northeast Newfoundland and Labrador.

Cape Island boat / Cape Islander

a boat used by inshore fishermen especially in Nova Scotia, with a high prow and a low stern. ❑ **Origin**: named after Cape Sable Island, NS, where first built in 1905.

coastal boat

(*Newfoundland*) a boat transporting supplies, mail, and some passengers to Newfoundland outports.

fishboat

(especially *BC*) a fishing boat.

jack boat

(*Newfoundland*) *historical* a small fishing schooner with two masts.

lake boat

a boat or ship designed for sailing on the Great Lakes.

log barge

(*BC*) a large barge used to transport logs from the log dump to the mill.

log bronc

(*BC*) a small tugboat used to direct a log boom or to gather logs together in the booming grounds.

mission boat

(*BC*) *historical* a vessel carrying spiritual and medical services to isolated villages on coastal inlets, inland rivers, etc.

Peterhead

(*North*) a decked launch or large whaleboat with a sail and a small motor, used in the eastern Arctic. ❑ **Origin**: Peterhead, Scotland, where early boats of this type were made.

pointer

a flat-bottomed rowboat, pointed at both ends and having a shallow draft, used by loggers especially in river drives.

rodney

(*Newfoundland*) a small fishing boat or punt.

trap skiff

(*Atlantic Canada*) a fishing boat used especially in the cod fishery.

umiak

a large, open, flat-bottomed boat made by stretching an animal hide over a wooden frame, traditionally used by Inuit women. ❑ **Pronunciation**: "OOMY ack".

York boat

historical a type of large, shallow-draft inland cargo boat used for transportation especially of furs and trade goods in the Prairies. ❑ **Origin**: York Factory, a remote historic site and trading depot in northeast Manitoba.

Aviation

bird dog
a small aircraft that acts as a spotter and guide for water bombers.

floatbase
a place on a river, lake, etc. where float planes dock.

NavCan
Nav Canada, a corporation responsible for providing air traffic control, flight information, weather briefings, airport advisory services and electronic aids to navigation for civil aviation in Canada.

seat sale
a sale of (especially) airline tickets at a reduced price.

sked
informal (*North*) a scheduled flight.

tundra tire
a wide airplane tire inflated to low pressure, used to operate from rough terrain.

water bomber
an aircraft used to drop water on forest fires, especially one which scoops up its load by skimming the surface of a lake etc.

Trains

colonist car
historical a railway car furnished with slatted wooden platforms for sitting or sleeping and equipped with a small stove.

harvest excursion
historical a low-priced train trip for workers travelling to the West to harvest crops.

Cars, Carriages, and Other Conveyances

Bennett buggy
an automobile hitched to horses or oxen, used during the Depression by owners who could no longer afford gasoline and operating expenses. ❏ **Origin**: named for R. B. Bennett, prime minister 1930–35.

Bombardier
proprietary an enclosed vehicle for travelling over snow or ice, driven by rear caterpillar treads and steered by front skis, and capable of carrying several passengers. ❏ **Pronunciation**: "bomba DEER". **Origin**: named for Armand Bombardier, who invented it and the Ski-Doo.

calèche
a two-wheeled one-horse vehicle with a seat for the driver on the splashboard, commonly used in tourist areas of Quebec. ❏ **Pronunciation**: "kuh LESH". **Origin**: French from Czech *kolesa* from *kolasa* "wheel carriage" from *kolo* "wheel".

carriole

historical **1** a horse-drawn sleigh with seats for a driver and often one or more passengers. **2** (*North*) *historical* a type of dogsled designed to carry a passenger or load in the front, with a rear platform for the driver to stand on. ❑ **Origin**: French from Italian *carriuola*, diminutive of *carro* "car".

cube van / cube truck

a truck resembling a van at the front, with a taller and wider cube-like storage compartment behind.

half-ton

a pickup truck with a carrying capacity of approximately half a ton.

Honda

proprietary (*North*) an all-terrain vehicle.

Red River cart

historical a sturdy two-wheeled wooden cart pulled by oxen or horses, used for transportation on the Prairies.

Ski-Doo

1 *proprietary* a snowmobile. **2** ride on a snowmobile.

Tundra Buggy

proprietary a large wheeled sightseeing bus used to take tourists into polar bear country.

Roads

autoroute
  an expressway in Quebec.

collector (lane)
  a lane running parallel to the express lanes of a freeway affording access between it and other roads.

concession (road)
  (*Ontario*) a rural road separating concessions (tracts of surveyed farmland).

core (lanes)
  the express lanes on a highway, usually separated by a guard-rail from the collector lanes.

grid (road)
  1 a road following the surveyed divisions of a township, municipality, etc. **2** (*Saskatchewan*) a road forming part of a provincial grid system constructed in the 1950s, with north-south roads one mile apart, and east-west roads two miles apart.

ice bridge
  a formation of ice across a river solid enough to support traffic.

ice road
  a winter road built across frozen lakes, rivers, muskeg, etc.

laneway

    a narrow urban street, especially behind houses or stores; a back alley.

plank road

    a road of planks laid across logs running end to end over rough ground.

road allowance

    a strip of land retained by government authorities for the construction of a road.

sideroad

    (*Ontario*) a rural road running perpendicular to a concession road.

trail

    (in Alberta) a major arterial road through a city.

Trans-Canada (Highway)

    a highway spanning Canada from St. John's to Victoria, formally opened in 1962 and completed in 1970.

trunk road

    an access road, especially one used for logging.

unassumed

    (of a road) not taken over for maintenance by a local authority; privately owned.

winter road

    (*North*) a secondary road made of compacted snow or ice, often plowed over a frozen lake or ground impassable in the summer.

On the Road (or Off)

advanced green

a flashing green traffic light in advance of the steady green light, indicating that oncoming traffic is halted.

gas bar

a gas station, especially one without a garage, consisting of a kiosk and pumps only.

green hornet

slang (in Ottawa and Toronto) a city employee who issues parking tickets. ❑ **Origin**: in reference to their green uniforms and their "stinging" of parking offenders.

parkade

a parking garage.

plug-in

an electrical outlet in a garage, near a parking space, etc. for plugging in the block heater of a car etc.

WHO WE ARE

Native Peoples
🍁 *Fun CanSpeak Facts:* Aboriginal Titles 🍁

Two Solitudes

The French Fact

I's the b'y

Immigration
Fun CanSpeak Facts:
🍁 Anyone for a Kubasa on Calabrese Sandwich? 🍁

Aboriginal Titles

Canada's Aboriginal peoples have had an undeniable impact on the language. Historically, we have borrowed and adapted many words from their languages, such as toboggan (literally "a device pulled by a cord", from Abenaki or Mi'kmaq), chipmunk ("who descends the tree headfirst", from Ojibwa), whisky jack ("black-smith", from Cree, because the bird is a sooty grey colour), sasquatch ("wild man", from Halkomelem), and igloo ("house", from Inuktitut).

But more recently too we have enriched our word stock with Aboriginal words, mostly self-designations preferred by various Aboriginal peoples to the names imposed on them by outsiders, either other Aboriginal groups or European newcomers. This phenomenon, which started with the shift from "Eskimo" to "Inuit" about thirty years ago, has affected all of Canada's Aboriginal peoples in the last fifteen years.

In some cases, the shift has been slight. For instance, the people traditionally known in English as the Micmac have in only the last ten years come to impose "Mi'kmaq" as the standard Canadian spelling of their name. But others are more complicated. The "new" word for the people traditionally known in Canada as the Ojibwa or the Ojibway (they are called the Chippewa in the US), is "Anishnabe". It means simply "people" in their language. We currently have examples of 40 different spellings for this word. But this pales in comparison with the numerous Aboriginal peoples living in BC. These people, traditionally known by such names as the Shuswap, Nanaimo, Carrier, and Thompson, have opted for spellings of their names that are very challenging for anglophones:

Secwepemc (formerly Shuswap)
Xne Nal Mewx (formerly Nanaimo)
Ktunaxa (formerly Kootenay)
Stl'atl'imx (formerly Lillooet)
Nlaka'pamux (formerly Thompson)

Other names which are somewhat less daunting, though still quite unusual, such as Nis'gaa and Nuu-chah-nulth (formerly Nootka) and Kwakwaka'wakw (formerly Kwakiutl), have caught on generally.

There has also been an influx of words designating Aboriginal cultural realities into more mainstream Canadian English. The term "Aboriginal title" has become part of our daily newspaper reading. But Aboriginal spiritual and cultural practices have impinged on our consciousness as well, so that words like "sweat lodge", "dream catcher", "sentencing circle", "vision quest", and "hoop dance", which might before have been found only in anthropological texts, are now very much part of general Canadian English. Many such words are not strictly speaking unique to Canada, since Aboriginal peoples in the United States may use them as well.

Aboriginal rights
rights enjoyed by a people by virtue of the fact that their ancestors inhabited an area from time immemorial.

Aboriginal title

the communal right of Aboriginal peoples to occupy and use the land inhabited by their ancestors from time immemorial.

adhesion

an addition made to a treaty when a new Aboriginal band signs it.

ancestral name

(among some West Coast Aboriginal groups, especially the Sne Nay Muxw) the personal name of an ancestor, conferred upon a child as a ceremonial name.

band

an Indian community officially recognized as an administrative unit by the federal government.

band council

a local form of Aboriginal government, consisting of a chief and councillors who are elected for two or three year terms to carry on band business.

beaver bundle

(especially among the Blackfoot) a medicine bundle containing the skin of a beaver and other objects.

comprehensive land claim

an Aboriginal land claim made on a usually large area of land which was never ceded or surrendered by treaty or purchase.

disc number

historical a number used in an identification system introduced in 1940 by the federal government in order to identify individual Inuit.

enfranchise

give up one's status as an Indian.

First Nation

an Indian band, or an Indian community functioning as a band but not having official band status.

First Nations

the Aboriginal peoples of Canada, not including the Inuit or Metis.

friendship centre

an institution established in a predominantly non-Aboriginal community to provide counselling and social services etc. to Aboriginal people.

Indian agent

historical a person appointed by the Department of Indian Affairs to supervise government programs on a reserve or in a specific region.

kokum / kookum

(among Cree, Ojibwa, and some Metis peoples) a grandmother.

land claim

a legal claim by an Aboriginal group concerning the use of an area of land.

Metis

a person of mixed Aboriginal and European descent.

non-status

designating a person of Indian ancestry who is not registered as an Indian under the Indian Act.

non-treaty

designating status or non-status Indian people who have not signed a treaty with the Canadian government.

numbered treaty

any of a number of land cession treaties signed from 1871 to 1921 between the Canadian government and Aboriginal nations throughout the north and west of Canada.

off-reserve

located on or inhabiting land which is not part of a designated reserve for Aboriginal people.

on-reserve

located on or inhabiting land which is part of a designated reserve for Aboriginal people.

residential school

historical a boarding school operated or subsidized by religious orders or the federal government to accommodate Aboriginal and Inuit students.

(land) scrip

historical a certificate issued to Metis entitling the bearer to 240 acres or money for the purchase of land, issued in compensation for lands lost by the Metis after the Northwest Rebellion.

shaking tent

(among some Algonquian peoples) a tent or lodge in which a shaman consulted the spirits for advice or assistance.

specific land claim

a land claim made against the federal government when specific treaty terms have not been met.

status

(of an Aboriginal person) registered as an Indian under the Indian Act.

sweat lodge

any of various structures heated by pouring water over hot stones, used by some Aboriginal groups to induce sweating, as for religious or medical purposes.

tikinagan

(among some North American Aboriginal peoples) a thin board to which an infant is strapped so that it can be transported on its mother's back or placed against a tree etc.

treaty

(in Canada and the US) an agreement between a government and a Native people in which the Native group ceded the rights to land in exchange for reserves, small cash payments, annual payments to band members, continued fishing and hunting rights, and other considerations. ❑ **take treaty** *historical* (of a Native group) agree to a treaty with the federal government.

treaty band

an Aboriginal band that has signed a treaty with the federal government.

treaty Indian

a status Indian who is a member of a treaty band.

treaty rights

the rights, e.g. that of holding land on a reserve, granted to a group of Aboriginal people under the terms of a treaty.

TWO SOLITUDES

allophone

(especially in Quebec) an immigrant whose first language is neither French nor English.

Anglo

informal an anglophone, especially in Quebec.

anglophone

an English-speaking person.

B & B / bi and bi

bilingualism and biculturalism.

Canuck

informal a Canadian.

Although its origins are obscure, the word is apparently derived from "Canada". Canadians are often puzzled to discover that American dictionaries label this word as "offensive" or "disparaging" and define it as applying specifically to French Canadians. None of this is true in Canadian usage, where "Canuck" is an affectionate self-designation.

francophone

a French-speaking person.

Johnny Canuck

1 a native, inhabitant, or citizen of Canada. **2** a Canadian soldier, especially during the world wars. **3** Canada personified.

two solitudes

the anglophone and francophone populations of Canada, portrayed as two cultures coexisting independent of and isolated from each other. ❑ **Origin**: from Hugh MacLennan's novel *Two Solitudes* (1945), depicting the conflict between anglophones and francophones.

unilingual

1 able to speak only one language. **2** spoken or written in or involving only one language.

 The pronunciation "yoona LING gyoo ull" (like "bye LING gyoo ull") is used only in Canada.

THE FRENCH FACT

In La Belle Province

fleur-de-lys

the flag of the province of Quebec, with a white cross and four white fleur-de-lys on an azure background. ❑ **Pronunciation**: "flurrda LEE" or "flurrda LEASE" (in French the latter pronunciation is used). **Origin**: The fleur-de-lys is a heraldic symbol which, though the word means literally "lily flower", is said to represent the iris. It was the emblem of the French monarchy and was being used as an emblem of Quebec by the 19th century.

francization

the establishment or adoption of French as the official or working language of business, education, etc.

indépendantiste

a person who supports the idea of Quebec independence; a sovereignist.

joual

a variety of Canadian French considered to be uneducated, characterized by non-standard grammar and syntax and, especially in cities, numerous English borrowings.

The word represents a pronunciation of the standard French *cheval* ("horse") found in many dialects of France. The expression *parler cheval*, meaning "speak badly" arose in early 19th-century informal French. In Quebec in the 1950s the phrase came to apply particularly to the Canadian French spoken by the working classes.

kétaine

in poor taste; tacky or kitschy. ❏ **Pronunciation**: "kay TEN".

language police

derogatory informal the officials of the Commission de Protection de la Langue Française responsible for ensuring that Quebec's language laws are enforced.

pure laine

designating a francophone Quebecer descended from the French settlers in New France and having exclusively French ancestry. ❏ **Origin**: French, literally = "pure wool".

Régie

any of several Quebec government bodies regulating insurance, housing, language, etc. ❏ **Origin**: French, = "government agency".

revenge of the cradle

the extremely high birth rate of French Canadians from the 19th to the mid-20th century, perceived as a means of retaliation against the English.

sign law

informal a Quebec provincial law regulating the use of languages other than French on signs.

sovereignist / sovereigntist

a supporter of Quebec's right to self-government; an adherent to the principle of sovereignty-association or full independence.

sovereignty-association

a proposed arrangement introduced in 1967 which would grant Quebec political independence while maintaining a formal especially economic association with the rest of Canada, including a shared currency. ❑ **Origin**: first used as the slogan of the Mouvement Souveraineté-Association, forerunners to the Parti Québécois.

tongue trooper

slang (in Quebec) a provincial government official responsible for enforcing the province's language laws, especially by monitoring commercial signs in stores, restaurants, etc.

The Legacy of the Acadians

aboiteau

a sluice gate in a dike, which allows flood water to flow out at low tide but does not allow sea water to enter. ❑ **Pronunciation**: "ab wah TOE". **Origin**: Acadian French, from Western French dialect *aboteau*, from Old French *bot* "dike", influenced by French *bois* "wood".

Acadian

1 a native or inhabitant of the former French colony of Acadia.
2 a francophone descendant of the early French settlers in Acadia.

Brayon

an inhabitant of the Madawaska region of northwestern New Brunswick, characterized by a mixed francophone and anglophone culture. ❑ **Origin**: from French *brayer* "break flax before spinning".

Expulsion

the eviction of the francophone Acadians between 1755 and 1762, when the British took over Acadia and forceably deported three-quarters of them to other parts of North America, especially Louisiana, where the name "Acadian" evolved into "Cajun".

fricot

a hearty Acadian stew containing potatoes and meat, fish, or seafood. ❑ **Pronunciation**: "free COE". **Origin**: French, "stew".

National Acadian Day

August 15, on which Acadians celebrate their culture and heritage.

ploye

a buckwheat pancake in Acadian cuisine. ❑ **Origin**: Acadian French, alteration of *plogue*, from English "plug", because of the heavy nature of the dish.

rappie pie

a savoury Acadian dish of Nova Scotia and PEI consisting of

grated potatoes and meat. ❑ **Origin**: Acadian French *pâté râpé* from *râper* "to grate".

tintamarre

a noisy parade, especially the annual celebration on National Acadian Day, August 15, involving a procession, the banging of pots and pans, playing of musical instruments, etc. ❑ **Pronunciation**: "tanta MAR". **Origin**: French, ="din".

I'S THE B'Y

Life on the Rock

blasty

(of a branch of a spruce or fir tree) dead and dry, with the needles (now brown or red) still attached.

crackie

a small, yappy dog of mixed breed.

duckish

dusk, twilight, or the time between sunset and dark.

jinker

a person who brings bad luck or who puts a jinx on someone or something. ❑ **Origin**: alteration of "jinx" + "-er".

landwash

the area along a shore between the high-water mark and the sea.

screech-in

a jocular ritual by which visitors to Newfoundland are "initi-ated", involving the drinking of screech and performing acts such as dipping a foot in the ocean, kissing a cod, etc.

People

bayman / baynoddy / baywop

an inhabitant of an outport, especially as opposed to someone living in a town.

hangashore

(*Atlantic Canada*) **1** a weak or sickly person. **2** an idle person, especially one regarded as too lazy to fish. ❏ **Origin**: Irish Gaelic *aindeiseoir* "weak, sickly person".

livyer

a resident or permanent settler in Newfoundland or Labrador.

outporter

an inhabitant or native of an outport.

Playtime

bazz

throw (a stone, marble, etc.).

copy

jump from one ice floe to the next in a game of follow-the-leader.

gale
> (of a child or animal) frolic or scamper playfully.

gawmoge
> **1** a clownish, mischievous person. **2** clownish or mischievous behaviour. ❑ **Pronunciation**: "ga MOAG". **Origin**: Irish *gamóg* "a clown or simpleton".

janny / mummer
> a costumed person who participates in group festivities and pranks at Christmas; a mummer. ❑ **Origin**: probably a variant of "johnny".

janny
> participate in mummering activities.

janny up
> dress up in a costume and mask to go mummering.

mummering / mumming
> the visiting of private houses by disguised merrymakers during the twelve days of Christmas.

Weather

airsome
> cold; invigorating.

civil
> (of the weather or sea) calm.

mauzy

(of weather) foggy, damp, or misty, especially producing condensation on objects. ❑ **Origin**: English dialect *mosey* "muggy, foggy".

Name That Seal

beater

a young harp seal, about three to four weeks old.

bedlamer

a young harp seal. ❑ **Origin**: possibly from "bedlam", a lunatic asylum, reflecting the apparently manic behaviour of the seals.

cat

a young or newborn seal.

patch

a herd of seals.

raggedy-jacket

a young harp seal whose coat is changing from pure white to brown and white.

square-flipper seal

an Arctic seal with large square flippers and a large mouth surrounded by beard-like bristles; a bearded seal.

swatch

an expanse of open water or ice, especially one inhabited by seals.

swile
　　archaic a seal.

IMMIGRATION

Anyone for a kubasa on calabrese sandwich?

Canada is a country of immigrants, and its multiculturalism has left its mark on the language. Take the influence of Ukrainian and Italian on Canadian English as just two examples.

Like all immigrants, Ukrainians and Italians were not considered prestige groups when they first arrived (the former starting in the 1880s and the latter in the years before the First World War). No doubt a Ukrainian-Canadian of that era would be astounded to come back to life in 2006 and discover that such Ukrainian words as "baba" (grandmother), "paska" (an Easter bread), "holubtsi" (cabbage rolls), "bandura" (a musical instrument), and not just one but three words referring to garlic sausage—"kubasa", "kubie", and "kubie burger"—are now included in a dictionary of Canadian English as fully integrated English words. But perhaps nothing would surprise our imaginary Ukrainian more than the entries for "gotch" and "gotchies", two well-entrenched slang words for underwear which are derived from a Ukrainian word for long johns. Mysteriously, in Alberta and BC, this word morphs into "gaunch" or "gaunchies".

Names for Italian food are common in all varieties of English. But some are unique to Canadian English. One is "panzerotto", the southern Italian version of what is more commonly known in English as a calzone. Another is "friulano" designating a mozzarella-like cheese typical of the Friuli region of Italy (Friulians constitute a significant proportion of Italian-Canadians). Interestingly, the cheese is not called "friulano" in Italy itself, but rather Montasio (or just "formaggio"!). There is also "calabrese" for a type of crusty bread. In British English, "calabrese" is a type of broccoli. Confusion could arise!

But perhaps the most interesting borrowing from Italian is not in fact a food word, though it sounds like it could be one. It is "mangia-cake", a derogatory term for Anglo-Canadians meaning literally "cake eater". The Italian-Canadian novelist Nino Ricci offers the explanation that it dates from the years after the Second World War, when Canada was experiencing a second large influx of Italian immigrants. It expresses the scorn of Italians for Canadian bread, which to them seemed so sweet as to be like cake. Another possible explanation is that Italian-Canadian immigrants found the Anglo habit of eating cake or pie with every meal so unlike their own dietary practices that it came to typify their new neigbours for them. A short form even exists. My nephew attended a high school in North Toronto, tellingly named "Dante Alighieri Academy", at which many of the students delighted in referring to him as a "cake". In recent years, the word "mangia-cake" has started to be used by non-Italians as well.

As Canadian society becomes ever more multicultural, we expect to see more borrowings from other languages as well. It will be interesting to see which of these are unique to Canadian English.

Africadian

a black Nova Scotian, especially a descendant of black Loyalists who settled in the province in the late 18th century or during the war of 1812.

astronaut

(*BC*) *informal* a (usually Asian) immigrant to Canada who commutes back to Hong Kong, Taiwan, etc. frequently to work, while leaving dependants resident in Canada.

courier parent

a person who obtains a visa to immigrate to Canada only so that his or her children may also immigrate.

immigration building / immigration hall / immigration shed

historical a building used to shelter new immigrants to the country until they found their own homes.

landed

denoting official recognition of immigration to Canada.

LINC

Language Instruction for Newcomers to Canada.

Maple Leaf Card

a plastic, wallet-sized Permanent Resident Card issued by the Canadian government from 2002 onwards.

Minister's Permit

a permit issued by a visa or immigration officer that allows a person not otherwise eligible to immigrate to Canada to enter or remain in Canada for a period of up to three years.

multicult

informal multicultural.

new Canadian

a person who has recently immigrated to Canada.

refugee determination (process)
the process by which the validity of a claim of refugee status is assessed.

settler's effects
items which a new immigrant is allowed to bring into Canada duty free.

visible minority
1 an ethnic group whose members are clearly racially distinct from those of the predominant race in a society. **2** a member of such an ethnic group.

WHERE
WE LIVE

Home Sweet Home
❦ *Fun CanSpeak Facts:* Our Home . . . and Native Language ❦

Places

Our Home . . . and Native Language

Thinking of buying a nice reno? How about designing a Château
style bunkie out of Tyndall stone for your cottage? Putting an
eavestrough on your century home? Javexing your Arborite
counters? Unknowingly, perhaps, you would be using distinctively Canadian words, of which there are many related to the
places in which we live.

Starting before the arrival of Europeans in Canada, there were
wigwams and longhouses and big houses and tipis. The Beothuk
in Newfoundland had mamateeks and the Inuit of course had
igloos.

Then the French arrived and gave us buildings with the characteristic "bellcast" or "coyau" roof of New France, with its curving,
ski-jump like profile.

The nineteenth century and early twentieth century witnessed
the construction of the famous railway hotels in what came to
be known as the Chateau style.

Skipping ahead to our own time, the spread of suburbia has seen
a plethora of backsplits and sidesplits, while those who prefer
to live downtown often do a reno on their century home, with a
favourite feature being the open-concept living-dining area. How
many of us realized that a word as ordinary as "open concept"

was uniquely Canadian? The Canadian roots of the "Vancouver special", however, are easily detectable. This style of house, common in Vancouver, has a low-pitched roof, a brick lower storey including bedrooms and a stucco upper storey with sliding glass doors from the living area opening onto a narrow, metal-railed balcony on the front of the house. Equally recognizable as Canadian is the "Lunenburg bump", a large bay window over the main entrance to a house peculiar to houses in Lunenburg.

And then there's the summer cottage. Or perhaps you call it a bungalow (Cape Breton), a shack (Newfoundland), a chalet or a country house (Quebec), a camp (northern Ontario and New Brunswick), a cabin (western Canada), or even "the lake" (Manitoba; invitees have to trust that there is actually a building there as well). Our predilection for cottages has also given us those distinctive features of the Muskoka cottage country, the bunkie or small outbuilding serving as a guest bedroom, and the Muskoka room, a sun room with windows on three sides. It might be a bit fanciful to have a miniature Chateau Frontenac as your guest accommodation at the lake, but it would be very Canadian. And if the famous architect Le Corbusier could describe grain elevators as "the cathedrals of the prairies", why couldn't you conceive of your bunkie as a chateau?

Finally, there are distinctively Canadian names for types of apartments. Has it ever occurred to you how odd non-Canadians must find it to see signs all over our cities advertising "Bachelors for Rent"? There are even wonderful variations on this, such as "Large Bachelor for Rent" and "Refurbished Bachelors Avail-able"! Although in other varieties of the language, a "bachelor apartment" is any apartment such as a bachelor might live in, in Canadian (and, surprisingly, South African English), it is specific-ally what the British would call a "bed-sitter". South Africans, however, do not use the shortened form "bachelor", so they don't rent bachelors as we do. In Quebec, they don't have bachelors either; they have "one-and-a-halfs". Whereas in the ROC, apartments are classified by the number of bedrooms, in Quebec, they use the number of rooms in total (the "half" being the bathroom). Another distinctive characteristic of rental housing in Quebec (and Ottawa) is that apartments are often advertised as being "heated and lighted" (a translation of the French *chauffé et éclairé*) whereas in the rest of the country the formula is likely to be "including heat and hydro".

So long as your home is not subjected to that bane of southwest Newfoundland, the "wreckhouse winds" (which I devoutly hope it isn't), you will also need to do some repairs to it, and, alas, the housework. Here too you will come across some uniquely Canadian words, many of them trade names used generically.

I was standing at the grocery checkout with a bottle of no-name bleach recently. "Do you want a bag for your Javex?" asked the cashier. It would strike any Canadian as absurd to say, "This isn't Javex, this is just bleach!", so ingrained is the generic use of this trade name in our linguistic makeup. Canadians even use "javex" as a verb, as in "I was javexing my undies".

Javex (pronounced jaVEX by many Newfoundlanders) has an interesting etymology. Bleach was known for a time as "Javel water", which was a translation of the French "eau de javel" which in turn comes from Javelle, a village, now part of Paris, where a solution of sodium hypochlorite was first used as bleach. In Quebec, you still sometimes see "Javel water" on bleach labels and in some texts whose writers are strongly influenced by French.

Now consider the predicament of this person:

"How many cans of Varsol it's going to take us before we get his fingers de-crazy-glued from his reading glasses is anybody's guess, but we won't give up until we finally free him."

Let's hope he doesn't crazy-glue himself in the States, where no one would know that Varsol is mineral spirits (the name, developed by Imperial Oil, is a blend of "varnish-maker's solvent").

While we're in the hardware department, imagine the perplexity of someone confronted with the problem of opening a crate fastened with Robertson screws without a Robertson screwdriver! The very efficient Robertson screwdriver was invented in the early 20th century by a businessman in Milton, Ontario, who had suffered an unfortunate blood-letting thanks to a standard slot screwdriver slipping out of a screwhead. Alas, our beloved "red Robertson" has not caught on widely outside of Canada.

Confusion could also be caused by another very common trade name, Arborite. The laminate used for countertops and tables is known only as Formica in other countries. In Britain, "Arborite" is a toxic substance that you put on tree stumps to cause them to rot. The British must wonder why Canadians have so much of it in their kitchens!

The Roofs Over Our Heads

bachelor
an apartment consisting of a single large room serving as bedroom and living room, with a separate bathroom.

bachelorette
a very small bachelor apartment.

backsplit

a house with floors raised half a storey at the rear, having an upper and lower main floor, and an upper and lower basement.

bellcast

a style of roof typical of traditional architecture in Quebec, with gables having the shape of a squared-off bell.

century home / century house

1 a house which is approximately one hundred years old. **2** any house designed or decorated in century-old styles.

Château style

a style of architecture derived from the French château, characterized by steep, often copper-covered, roofs and round towers, used especially in building railway hotels in Canada in the early 20th century.

cottage

(*Quebec*) a small, two-storey house in the city.

coyau

(*Quebec*) a steep roof design having wing-like gables to channel runoff snow and ice; a bellcast roof. Pronounced "COY oh".
❑ **Origin**: French from Old French *coe* from Latin *cauda*, "tail".

efficiency unit

a hotel room or small apartment with limited washing and cooking facilities.

greystone

1 grey stones used in building walls, houses, etc. **2** a house etc. made of greystone.

Lunenburg bump

a large bay window over the main entrance to a house, peculiar to houses in Lunenburg, NS.

Muskoka room

(*Southern Ontario*) a glassed (or screened) room on the side of a house, cottage, etc.

one-and-a-half, two-and-a-half, etc.

(*Quebec*) an apartment having one (two, etc.) room(s) plus a bathroom.

open concept

(of a house, office, etc.) having few or no internal walls or partitions.

quadruplex

a building divided into four self-contained residences.

raised bungalow

a bungalow with the main floor raised to allow the basement to be partly above ground level.

sidesplit

a split-level house having floors raised half a level on one side thus having an upper and lower basement and an upper and lower main floor.

Vancouver special

(*BC*) a style of house common in Vancouver having a low-pitched roof, a brick lower storey including the bedrooms and a stucco upper storey with sliding glass doors from the living area opening onto a narrow, metal-railed balcony on the front of the house.

Not Quite Roughing it in the Bush

bungalow

(*Cape Breton*) a summer cottage, especially a modest one.

bunkie / bunkhouse

(*Southern Ontario*) a small outbuilding on the property of a summer cottage providing extra sleeping accommodation for guests.

caboose

a portable wooden cabin, especially one on runners which can be pulled over snow.

camp

(*Northern Ontario, Maritimes*) a summer cottage.

chalet

(*Quebec*) a holiday cottage.

cottage country

an area in which there are many cottages.

country house

(*Quebec*) a summer cottage.

shack

(*Atlantic Canada*) a dwelling used for vacation purposes, usually located in a rural area near a lake or river.

Not Freezing in the Dark

CANDU

proprietary a nuclear reactor using easily replaceable fuel bundles and a heavy water cooling and moderating system.
❑ **Origin**: Acronym from "Canada" + "deuterium" + "uranium".

hydro

1 electricity. **2** an electric utility company.

insulbrick

simulated-brick asphalt siding used on houses etc.

pot light

an interior light encased in a cylindrical shell, mounted recessed into a ceiling.

Quebec heater

a tall, cylindrical stove using coal or wood for fuel, used especially for heating or cooking.

R-2000

a certification designating houses built to a very high standard of energy efficiency, indoor air quality, and environmental impact. ❑ **Origin**: "R" representing "resistance to heat loss".

trilight

a light bulb that can be adjusted to shine at any of three degrees of brightness.

Yukon stove

(*North*) a simple stove used for cooking and heating, often consisting of an oil drum on legs.

Furniture

chesterfield

a couch or sofa.

> "Chesterfield" has long been considered a shibboleth of Canadian English. Although other varieties of English use the word, they do so to designate a sofa with the arms the same height as the back, whereas in Canada it means any kind of sofa. Some studies suggest the word is dying out (or already dead) amongst younger urban speakers, being replaced by "couch", but there is plenty of evidence to prove that it is still very much alive.

Muskoka chair

a slatted wooden lawn chair with a fan-shaped back and broad arms.

Toronto couch

(especially *West*) a Winnipeg couch.

Winnipeg couch

a couch with no arms or back, which converts into a double bed.

Home hardware

Arborite

proprietary a plastic laminate used in countertops, tables, etc.

Ardox nail

proprietary a type of nail with a spiral shaft.

Frost fence

proprietary a chain-link fence.

Gyproc

proprietary drywall. ❑ **Origin**: blend of "gypsum" + "rock".

Javex

proprietary chlorine bleach. ❑ **Origin**: from "Javel water", from French *eau de javel*, from *Javelle*, a village, now part of greater Paris, where sodium hypochlorite solution was first used as bleach.

reno

informal **1** a renovated house. **2** renovation.

Robertson screw / Robertson screwdriver

1 a type of screw with a square notch on the head. **2** a type of screwdriver with a square tip designed to fit into a Robertson screw. ❑ **Origin**: P. L. Robertson, Canadian businessman, d.1950.

snake (rail) fence

a fence of stacked roughly-split logs laid in a zigzag pattern with ends overlapping at an angle.

Tyndall stone

a variety of mottled dolomitic limestone quarried near Winnipeg, noted for the presence of a large number of fossils. ❑ **Origin**: after the town of Tyndall, where it is quarried, named after John Tyndall, the Irish physicist who first explained why the sky is blue.

Varsol

proprietary mineral spirits, a volatile liquid distilled from petroleum and used especially as a paint thinner. ❑ **Origin**: blend of "varnish makers'" + "solvent".

whitepainting

the renovation or reclamation of a house, building, or neighbourhood in a derelict part of a city's urban core.

PLACES

From Far and Wide

across

(*PEI*) in or to Nova Scotia or New Brunswick.

away

(*Atlantic Canada*) in a place other than the speaker's home province or Atlantic Canada in general.

Baffinland

the area of the Canadian Arctic including Baffin Island and adjoining islands and mainland and the eastern High Arctic islands.

banana belt

informal the Niagara Peninsula or southern BC.

the Barrens / Barren Grounds / Barren Lands

the treeless, sparsely populated region of northern Canada, lying between Hudson Bay and Great Slave and Great Bear lakes.

Boston States

(*Maritimes* & *Nfld*) New England.

down-island

(*BC*) to or in a more southerly part of Vancouver Island.

(Eastern) Townships

a region of south central Quebec, lying between the St. Lawrence and the US border, and Montreal and Quebec City.

French Shore

1 an informal name for the district of Clare, a French-Acadian area along the rocky southwestern coast of Nova Scotia, north of Yarmouth. **2** *hist.* that part of the coastline of the island of Newfoundland where the French were granted fishing rights until 1904. It stretched around the island from Cape Bonavista to Cape Ray.

go down the road

leave one's hometown in search of employment, adventure, etc., especially leave the Maritimes for central or western Canada.

the Great White North

jocular Canada.

High Arctic

the part of the Canadian Arctic that lies within the Arctic Circle.

inside

(*North*) within the Yukon, Northwest Territories, or Nunavut.

keystone province

the province of Manitoba. ❑ **Origin**: from the shape of its outline on a map.

(La) Belle Province

the province of Quebec.

La-La Land

informal a nickname for British Columbia.

last best West

a nickname for the Canadian prairies in promotional literature attracting homesteaders in the early 1900s.

Lotus Land

jocular southern British Columbia.

Low Arctic

the part of the Canadian Arctic south of the Arctic Circle.

Near North

the southern edge of the Subarctic, extending across Canada in a band just north of the heavily settled areas of the Fraser Valley, the Prairies, and Southern Ontario and the St. Lawrence Valley.

north of 60

informal the areas of Canada north of 60 degrees latitude, especially the Yukon, Northwest Territories, and Nunavut.

outside

(*North*) in or to the rest of the world outside the Territories, especially a more heavily populated or urban area.

ROC

the parts of Canada outside the province of Quebec; the "rest of Canada".

The Rock

the island of Newfoundland.

Shield country

the area covered by the Canadian Shield, characterized by thin soil, rock outcrops, countless lakes and rivers, and, in the southern areas, vast coniferous forests.

Sixty

the parallel of latitude 60 degrees north of the equator as forming the boundary between the western provinces to the south and the territories to the north.

south of 60

the areas of Canada south of 60 degrees latitude, especially the ten provinces south of the Yukon, Northwest Territories, and Nunavut.

Spud Island

informal Prince Edward Island.

Sunshine Coast

an informal name for the area along the southwestern coast of BC, north of Howe Sound on the Strait of Georgia. ❑ **Origin**: with reference to the bright and pleasant weather along this section of the coast.

the True North

Canada.

24 Sussex Drive

the official residence of the prime minister in Ottawa, since 1951.

upalong

(*Newfoundland*) to or on a location away from a person or place, especially to or on mainland Canada.

up-island

(*BC*) towards or of the northern or more remote parts of Vancouver Island.

Upper Canada

(*Maritimes*) Ontario.

uptown

the central business district, especially of a small town.

Nicknames for cities

Cowtown

Calgary.

Cradle of Confederation

Charlottetown.

Edmonchuk

Edmonton. ❑ **Origin**: blend of "Edmonton" + -*chuk*, a common suffix in Ukrainian surnames, reflecting the high proportion of Ukrainian Canadians in Edmonton.

Fat City

Ottawa. ❑ **Origin**: referring to its cushy and stable bureaucratic economy.

Hogtown

Toronto. ❑ **Origin**: perhaps with reference to the city's expanding farmers' markets and livestock trading during the early 19th century.

the Jaw

Moose Jaw.

the Lakehead

Thunder Bay.

P.A.

Prince Albert.

the Peg

Winnipeg.

the Queen City

1 Regina. **2** Toronto.

St. Kitts

St. Catharines.

Saskabush

Saskatoon.

Scarberia

Scarborough, Ontario.

the Soo

Sault Ste. Marie.

Steel City

1 Hamilton, Ontario. **2** Sydney, Nova Scotia.

Steeltown

Hamilton.

T.O.

Toronto. ❑ **Origin**: abbreviation of "Toronto, Ontario".

Tuk

Tuktoyaktuk.

Winterpeg

a jocular nickname for Winnipeg.

WHAT
WE WEAR

Clothes
❦ *Fun CanSpeak Facts:* Bundle Up! ❦

Accessories

Bundle Up!

Our accoutrements. Why do we call them what we do? Of course we have to start with the toque (or tuque). "Toque", when it is used to mean what the British hilariously (to us, anyway) call a "bobble hat", is a Canadianism, and it has a Canadian history. English Canadians borrowed from Canadian French the word *tuque*, which then got confused with another French word designating a kind of headgear, the "toque". That tall white hat worn by chefs is a "toque" (the word comes from an Italian name for a kind of silk fabric) but it wouldn't be much good at keeping your ears warm. Most dictionaries, not being Canadian, define the word "toque" as a "small brimless hat, made of velvet, and worn by women", and say it is pronounced, not "tuke", but "toke" (woe betide the new Canadian shopping for one!). Some dictionaries even provide a helpful drawing of an Elizabethan lady wearing a cute puffy hat with a feather sticking out of it. Pity the poor non-Canadian who tries to apply this definition when reading a Canadian novel that includes lines like "they were dressed like loggers in toques and boots". Visions of crossdressing lumberjacks spring to mind. Our "toque" ultimately comes from a very old pre-Roman word meaning a hill or gourd, which remained alive in some French dialects and was brought over to North America, where it became "tuque" (as in the name of the town La Tuque in Quebec). It is probably because of the similarity in shape between a hill and the knitted cap that they adopted this word for what we use it for today.

Keeping our various body parts warm is obviously a priority. Losing our mitts in the middle of the winter could be disastrous, and that's why our children need "idiot strings" (we owe the idea, though not the word, to the Inuit). We also have a large number of words for coats and sweaters, including the delightful Saskatchewanism "bunny hug", for a hooded sweatshirt. Why some Canadians see bunnies where others see kangaroos is a mystery.

Have you ever worn your Sudbury dinner jacket with your Nipigon nylons? These are slang terms in Northern Ontario for a lumberjack jacket and heavy grey work socks (the latter are also known as "pit socks" in the coal-mining-influenced vocabulary of Cape Breton). Perhaps that outfit (with some Stanfields underneath to keep us toasty) with a toque and idiot strings should be the official Canadian uniform.

Underwear

gaunch
> (especially *BC* & *Alberta*) *slang* underwear. ❑ **Origin**: alteration of "gotch".

gitch
> *slang* underwear.

gotch / gotchies
> *slang* underpants. ❑ **Origin**: probably Ukrainian.

Stanfields
> *proprietary* men's underwear, especially long underwear. ❑ **Origin**: Stanfield's Ltd., an underwear manufacturer in Truro, NS.

Footwear

cork boot

    (*BC*) a logger's boot with spiked soles. ❑ **Origin**: "Cork" represents a pronunciation of "caulk" meaning "a spike", a word which is ultimately from the Latin word *calcar* meaning "a spur", from *calx* meaning "heel".

kamik

    a traditional Inuit boot made from seal or caribou skin.

logan

    (*Newfoundland*) a leather boot with a rubber foot, reaching to below the knee, worn in winter or when working in the bush.

mukluk

    a traditional Inuit boot, usually made from seal or caribou skin. ❑ **Origin**: Yupik *maklak* "bearded seal".

pit socks

    (*Cape Breton*) standard grey work socks, especially worn by miners.

rubbers

    (*Newfoundland*) long, waterproof boots worn especially by fishermen and sealers.

runner / running shoe

    any of various shoes having an upper made of nylon, canvas, etc. and a rubber or synthetic sole.

snowmobile boot

    a high, heavy snow boot worn especially when snowmobiling.

toe rubber

one of a pair of galoshes that extends from the heel of a man's shoe under the sole and over the tip of the toe.

Coats, Jackets, and Sweaters

amautik / packing parka

(*North*) an Inuit woman's parka with a large hood in which a child may be carried.

atigi

(*North*) a type of Inuit parka, made especially from caribou skin, with the fur on the inside, worn either on its own or as the inner layer of a double-layered parka. ❏ **Pronunciation**: "AT ug ee" or "a TEEG ee". **Origin**: Inuktitut, from *attike* "covering".

blanket coat

a coat made from a blanket or blanket cloth, especially Hudson's Bay blanket cloth.

bunny hug

(*Saskatchewan*) a hooded sweatshirt.

bush jacket

a jacket, usually of warm, red and black checked material, originally worn by loggers; a lumberjack jacket.

cossack

(*Newfoundland*) a hooded pullover made of animal skin or heavy cotton. ❏ **Origin**: alteration of "cassock".

Cowichan sweater

a heavy sweater of homespun, undyed wool with various patterns of animals, birds, fish, whales, etc., produced by the Coast Salish of the Cowichan valley on Vancouver Island.

hockey jacket

an outer jacket, usually of nylon with a quilted lining, with a hockey team's crest on the chest and the owner's name, position, number, etc. embroidered on the arm.

kangaroo jacket

a hooded sweatshirt with a front pouch.

Mother Hubbard

a type of woman's parka, worn especially in the Western Arctic, consisting of an inner duffle shell covered in a bright print fabric, edged with fur at the hood and cuffs and having a deep ruffle around the bottom.

Siwash sweater

(*West*) a thick woollen sweater decorated with symbols or animals from Aboriginal mythology. ❏ **Pronunciation**: "SIGH wash". ❏ **Origin**: Chinook Jargon, from Canadian French *sauvage*.

sunburst

a trimming of fur around the hood of a parka.

Gloves and Mittens

garbage mitt

(*Manitoba*) *slang* a thickly padded deerskin mitt. ❏ **Origin**: so called because typically worn by garbagemen in the winter.

idiot string

a string attached to each of two mittens or gloves and strung through the sleeves and across the inside back of a child's coat, to prevent the mittens etc. from being lost.

nipper

(*Atlantic Canada*) a glove worn while handling lines to protect the hands from friction.

Hats

Cape Ann

(*Newfoundland*) a broad-brimmed rain hat with an extended back flap. ❏ **Origin**: Cape Ann in Massachusetts.

Christie stiff / Christy stiff

historical a derby hat. ❏ **Origin**: probably from Christy & Co., English hat manufacturer.

Mountie hat

the characteristic tan hat of the RCMP, with a dimpled crown and broad flat encircling brim.

Pangnirtung hat

(*North*) a knitted wool hat in bright colours, with a tassel at the crown and earflaps, traditional in the Eastern Arctic. ❏ **Origin**: Pangnirtung, a hamlet on Baffin Island.

toque / tuque

1 a close-fitting knitted hat, often with a tassel or pompom on the crown. **2** a long knitted stocking cap.

Belt

arrow sash / Assomption sash / ceinture fléchée / Metis sash / voyageur sash

historical a long, brightly coloured sash woven with an arrow-shaped pattern and worn around the waist, especially by voyageurs.

Jewellery

ammolite

the brilliantly coloured opalescent fossilized shell of an ammonite, found only in southern Alberta, used as a precious gem. ❑ **Origin**: "ammonite" (a fossilized mollusc) + the suffix "-lite" used in mineral names.

Iron Ring

a ring made of iron or stainless steel worn on the little finger by graduating engineers who have undergone a special ritual involving a statement of their commitment to the highest professional standards.

It is commonly believed that the first rings were made from the steel girders of the Quebec Bridge which collapsed in 1907 with much loss of life, to remind engineers of their duties and responsibilities. This story is not true (the ceremony involving the rings was instituted in 1925), though the Iron Ring does serve as a symbolic reminder of the engineer's obligations to society.

Blankets

button blanket

a colourful blanket elaborately ornamented with mother-of-pearl, traditionally worn by leaders of Aboriginal peoples of the Pacific Coast of North America.

Chilkat blanket

a pentagonal ceremonial blanket worn by West Coast Aboriginal peoples, woven from mountain goat hair and shredded cedar bark and covered with symbolic designs in yellow, blue, black, and white.

Hudson's Bay blanket

a durable woollen blanket woven in a variety of patterns, including cream with wide stripes of green, red, yellow, and indigo, and scarlet or green with black stripes.

point blanket

a type of Hudson's Bay blanket with distinctive markings or "points", usually in the form of short black lines, woven in to indicate weight.

EAT, DRINK, AND BE MERRY

Food, Glorious Food!
🍁 *Fun CanSpeak Facts:* Canadian English—A Real Mouthful 🍁

Drinking and Carousing
🍁 *Fun CanSpeak Facts:* Drink Canada dry! 🍁

Canadian English—A Real Mouthful

Cape Breton pork pies contain no pork, bumbleberry pie contains no bumbleberries, Digby chicken is not chicken, and CPR strawberries are not strawberries: are Canadians hopelessly confused when it comes to naming items of food?

Canadians will probably be surprised to know how many uniquely Canadian names for food there are. "Nanaimo bar" or "Montreal smoked meat" or "Winnipeg goldeye" are easily identifiable as Canadian, but did you know that asking for Boston bluefish in an American grocery store (even in Boston) would cause confusion? Not half as much confusion, mind you, as asking for an "all-dressed" pizza!

And then there's the humble butter tart, a classic of our mothers' cooking since the beginning of the century. Hard as it may be to believe, other nations manage to live without butter tarts! And neither do they have date squares, which are also known in Western Canada as "matrimonial cake".

In fact, you will find that some foods go by very different names as you travel across the country. Take that staple of the Canadian diet, the round, sugar-coated, jam-filled doughnut. A "jelly doughnut" in BC and almost everywhere east of Thunder Bay (except in parts of Nova Scotia, where it can also be called a "Burlington bun"). But it's known as a "jambuster" throughout northwestern Ontario and Manitoba, and even as far west as Moose Jaw. Venture further into Saskatchewan and Alberta and it becomes a "bismarck". Just to add to the confusion, Manitobans do use the word "bismarck", but they mean a cream-filled doughnut with a chocolate glaze . . . which is called a "Boston cream" in southern Ontario.

The word "dainties" is also a potential source of regional confusion. In Western Canada, it is used collectively to designate an assortment of small cakes, squares, and tarts served at social gatherings. Newly arrived in Ontario, I announced one day to a friend that I was planning to take some dainties to a shower. Only his look of total bewilderment alerted me to the fact that he thought I was planning to take some frilly ladies' underwear into the bathroom!

Many food terms in Canadian English have been borrowed from other languages; no slouches at appreciating another culture's mouth-watering delicacies, we borrow the word along with the food itself. So we have "panzerotto" from Italian, "holubtsi" (cabbage rolls) from Ukrainian, "pemmican" from Cree, "perogies" from Polish, and "tourtiere" and "poutine" (some might admittedly dispute that this concoction of french fries, cheese curds, and gravy is a "delicacy") from French. There are actually two types of poutine: in Acadia it is a kind of dumpling made with grated potatoes. The better known poutine, which has spread throughout Canada, comes from Quebec. No one really knows where the word comes from originally; one theory suggests that it is actually a corruption of the word "pudding". But it's more likely that it comes from a French dialect word meaning a dish made of odd scraps of this and that.

Some wonderfully evocative words have also been created out of the existing English word stock. In Nova Scotia, a blueberry grunt is a hearty dessert of berries topped with a dense cakelike dough. A Newfoundland delicacy is flipper pie, which is indeed made with flippers—seal flippers, that is.

Newfoundland, in fact, is a whole culinary adventure unto itself. Bangbelly is a dense pudding or cake made of cooked rice, flour, molasses, raisins, salt pork, and spices. Pork buns are tea biscuits made with salt pork and served with molasses. Lassy bread is a sweet yeast bread with molasses, raisins, and spices (probably served with salt pork). These are in addition to the classic Newfoundland dish: fish and brewis, which is salt cod soaked with hardtack and served with (you probably have guessed it by now) molasses and salt pork. Newfoundlanders' fondness for molasses is reflected in their name for it: "lassy", which we Canadian dictionary editors were recently delighted to see turn up in the name of a new President's Choice brand cookie, "lassy mogs" on sale across the nation.

What about that stereotypically Canadian food, back bacon or peameal bacon (something the Americans call "Canadian bacon")? Have you ever wondered why it's called peameal, since it's actually coated in cornmeal? Cured meats like this used to be given a coating of ground dried peas, but corn is so abundant in North America that it became the preferred coating.

Still wondering about those apparently misnamed dishes? Cape Breton pork pies are date-filled tarts with a rich pastry, often topped with icing; they look a little like a classic pork pie. Bumbleberry pie contains a mixture of fruits, usually blackberries, raspberries, blueberries, and strawberries, sometimes also apples and rhubarb. The combination has really caught on in the last ten years. Now you can get bumbleberry yogourt, bumbleberry jam, and bumbleberry granola bars as well as the classic pie. The word comes to us, possibly via Newfoundland, from an English dialect word meaning rosehip or blackberry. Digby chicken is cured or dried herring in Nova Scotia. "CPR strawberries" is a jocular term formerly used in more remote areas for prunes or dried apples.

Fruits and Vegetables

bakeapple / baked-apple berry
(*Atlantic Canada*) a low-growing plant of the raspberry family with an edible amber fruit; a cloudberry. ❑ **Origin**: corruption of Inuktitut *appik* + "apple".

CPR strawberries
informal jocular prunes or dried apples.

Fameuse / Snow Apple
a variety of apple grown especially in Quebec from the 17th to the 19th century. ❑ **Origin**: called a "Snow Apple" because of the whiteness of its flesh.

fiddlehead greens
the young, curled, edible fronds of certain ferns.

jellied salad
a sweet or savoury dish made of fruit or chopped vegetables in fruit-flavoured gelatin.

marshberry
(*Newfoundland*) a creeping cranberry of sphagnum bogs with small edible pink to purple berries; a bog cranberry.

Melba

an early, sweet, yellow cooking and eating apple with pink and red stripes. ❑ **Origin**: named in honour of the Australian opera singer Dame Nellie Melba.

Norland

a large, red and green cooking and eating apple, originally developed in Saskatchewan. ❑ **Origin**: probably from "Northland", with reference to the cultivar's suitability for northern climates.

pepper squash

a variety of winter squash with dark green to orange ridged skin and yellow flesh.

poutine

1 a dish of french fries topped with cheese curds and a sauce, usually gravy. **2** (in Acadian cuisine) **a** a potato dumpling. **b** a pudding or pie.

Pronounced "poo TEEN". Acadian poutine predates the Québécois poutine by about a century. The ultimate origin of this word beyond Canadian French is uncertain. It is probably derived from various similar words in many French dialects, and influenced by the English word "pudding". The story behind the french fries and cheese curds concoction is that Fernand Lachance, a snack bar owner in Warwick, Quebec, when asked by a customer in 1957 to combine fries and cheese in a bag, told him it would be a "maudite poutine" (a hell of a mess), but the combination and the word stuck.

saskatoon

(*Prairies*) a species of the serviceberry, found abundantly in western Canada and bearing a sweet purple berry. ❑ **Origin**: Derived from the Cree word *misaskwatomin*, interpreted as "fruit of the tree of many branches". "Saskatoon" designates one species of the plant called a Juneberry or shadbush elsewhere.

soopollalie

(*BC*) soapberry, a type of buffalo berry which contains small amounts of saponin, a substance that foams in water. Pronounced "SOAP a lally". ❑ **Origin**: from *soop*, variant of "soap" + Chinook Jargon *olallie* "berry".

Spartan

a medium- or large-sized red eating or cooking apple with tiny white dots, bred to withstand relatively cold winters.

spits

(*West*) *informal* sunflower seeds.

squashberry

the edible fruit of several North American viburnums, used to make jam; a lowbush cranberry.

Yellow Transparent

an early yellow-skinned apple used for cooking and eating.

Stews, Casseroles, and Savoury Pies

boiled dinner

(*Atlantic Canada*) a dish of meat and vegetables, especially beef brisket, potatoes, cabbage and root vegetables, stewed together in water.

brewis

(*Newfoundland*) a stew made of hardtack soaked in water and boiled. Pronounced "brooze". ❑ **Origin**: English dialect "bread soaked in fat or broth", from Old French *bro(u)ez* "broth", ultimately from Germanic.

cipaille

a deep pie with alternating layers of meat and pastry. ❏ **Pronunciation**: "sea PIE". **Origin**: This word was in fact borrowed into Canadian French in the early 20th century from the English word "sea pie" which had designated a savoury pie with multiple layers of pastry since the 1700s.

colcannon

(*Newfoundland*) a dish of various vegetables, usually including cabbage, traditionally eaten on Halloween. ❏ **Origin**: Gaelic *cal ceannan,* literally "white-headed cabbage", from Latin *caulis* "cabbage" + Old Irish *ceann* "head".

fèves au lard

(*Quebec*) baked beans with pork. ❏ **Pronunciation**: "fevv oh LAR".

fish and brewis

(*Newfoundland*) a dish of salt cod and hardtack soaked in water and then fried and garnished with fried salt pork.

fricot

(*Maritimes*) a hearty Acadian stew containing potatoes and meat, fish, or seafood. ❏ **Pronunciation**: "free COE". **Origin**: French, "stew".

hodgepodge

(*Maritimes*) a dish of potatoes and other vegetables cooked in milk and butter.

holubtsi

(*Prairies*) cabbage rolls. ❏ **Pronunciation**: "HOL up chee". **Origin**: Ukrainian.

Jiggs' dinner

(*Newfoundland*) a boiled dinner of corned beef, potatoes, and other vegetables, especially cabbage.

panzerotto

a baked pizza-like turnover, consisting of dough folded into a sealed pocket, filled with tomato sauce, cheese, etc. ❑ **Origin**: Italian *panzarotto* from *panza*, obsolete form of *pancia* "belly", from its shape.

pease pudding

(*Newfoundland*) dried split peas boiled in a pudding bag (often in the pot containing meat boiling for Jigg's dinner), mashed and seasoned with butter, salt, and pepper when cooked.

rappie pie

a savoury Acadian dish of Nova Scotia and PEI consisting of grated potatoes and meat. ❑ **Origin**: Acadian French *pâté râpé* from *râper* "to grate".

(seal) flipper pie

(*Newfoundland*) a pie with a filling of seal flippers.

sea pie

a dish of especially leftover meat and vegetables stewed and baked in a crust.

Solomon Gundy / Solomon Grundy

(*Nova Scotia*) a dish of salted herring marinated in vinegar, pickling spices, sugar, and onions. ❑ **Origin**: corruption of "salmagundi", a dish of chopped meat, anchovies, eggs, onions, etc., and seasoning, from French *salmigondis* "game stew", from *sel* "salt" + *condir* "seasoning".

tourtière

a French-Canadian meat pie consisting especially of ground pork and spices with a flaky double crust, traditionally served at Christmas. ❏ **Pronunciation**: "tor TYAIR". **Origin**: Canadian French from French dialect, = "pie dish".

Meat and Fish

banquet burger

a hamburger with bacon and cheese.

canner

(*Maritimes*) a lobster designated for canning because it is too small for the market.

cod tongue

(*Newfoundland*) the tongue of a codfish, fried in pork fat and eaten as a delicacy.

cottage roll

a pickled, boneless, prepared ham from the pork butt.

country food

game, fish, or other foods that can be obtained while in the bush.

cretons

(*Quebec*) a spread of shredded pork cooked with onions in pork fat. ❏ **Origin**: Canadian French probably from Middle Dutch *kerte* "cut".

cutlette

a roughly oval-shaped, breaded patty of finely chopped meat.

Digby chicken / Digby chick

(*Maritimes*) a dried or cured herring. ❏ **Origin**: after Digby, Nova Scotia.

farmer's sausage

seasoned raw pork sausage in a casing but not in links, especially of German origin.

kubasa

a garlic sausage of Ukrainian origin. ❏ **Origin**: corruption of Ukrainian *kovbasa*, "sausage".

kubie

(*Alberta*) kubasa, especially when eaten on a hot dog bun.

kubie burger

(*Alberta*) kubasa pressed into a patty and eaten on a bun, like a hamburger.

lobster roll

(*Maritimes*) a long bread roll with a filling of chopped lobster and mayonnaise.

(Montreal) smoked meat

cured beef similar to pastrami but more heavily smoked.

muktuk

a traditional Inuit food consisting of the skin and surface blubber of a whale, especially a beluga or narwhal, either dried, cooked, or eaten raw.

nip

(*Manitoba & Northwestern Ontario*) a hamburger.

The word is particularly associated with the Salisbury House chain of restaurants, which started using "Salisbury Nips" as a name for sandwiches and hamburgers in 1931 and registered it as a tradename in 1933.

peameal bacon

back bacon rolled in a coating of fine cornmeal. ❏ **Origin**: from the former practice of coating cured meats in a meal of ground dried peas.

Pogo

proprietary a hot dog covered in cornmeal batter, deep-fried or baked, and served on a stick.

scruncheons

(*Newfoundland*) small pieces of pork fat or fatback fried to a crisp and usually eaten with fish and brewis. ❏ **Origin**: perhaps related to English dialect "scrunchings" = "table scraps".

shore lunch

a meal cooked on a lakeshore or riverbank etc. as part of a fishing trip or other boating excursion, featuring freshly caught fish, pan-fried.

side bacon

bacon from the belly of a pig, having alternate strips of fat and lean.

side ribs

a cut of pork from the belly including the ribs and adhering meat.

smokie

a sausage or hot dog.

steakette

a thin patty of ground beef, meant to be cooked quickly.

steamie

(*Quebec*) a steamed hot dog.

toupie

a round boneless smoked ham. ❏ **Pronunciation**: "TOO pee".
Origin: perhaps from French, *toupie* = "spinning top", because
of its shape.

Breads, Cereals, and Pancakes

bannock

a bread similar to tea biscuits, made of flour, water, and fat,
sometimes leavened with baking powder, and cooked on a
griddle or over a fire.

calabrese

a round white crusty Italian bread. ❏ **Pronunciation**: "kala
BRAY zee". **Origin**: Italian = "Calabrian".

hard bread

(*Newfoundland*) a thick, oval biscuit baked without salt and
dried in a kiln.

lassy bread

(*Newfoundland*) a sweet yeast bread with molasses, raisins,
and spices.

Montreal bagel

a type of bagel, originally made in Montreal, which is lighter, thinner, and sweeter than other kinds of bagels.

paska

a rich, usually decorated, egg bread, often containing dried fruits, traditional at Easter among people of Ukrainian origin. ❑ **Origin**: Ukrainian, literally "Easter".

ploye

a buckwheat pancake in Acadian cuisine. ❑ **Origin**: Acadian French, alteration of *plogue*, from English "plug", because of the heavy nature of the dish.

pönnukökur

an originally Icelandic crepe made with eggs, sugar, and milk, often served sprinkled with both white and brown sugar and rolled. ❑ **Pronunciation**: "pawna COOKER".

pork bun

(*Newfoundland*) a tea biscuit with finely chopped salt pork as an ingredient.

Red River Cereal

proprietary a mixture of cracked wheat, cracked rye, and flax seeds, served cooked as a hot cereal.

60% whole wheat

designating bread, crackers, etc. made with a proportion of 60% whole wheat flour and 40% white flour.

tea biscuit

a small baked foodstuff, leavened with baking powder or soda, often containing raisins or currants; a scone.

tea bun

(*Newfoundland*) a tea biscuit.

Garnishes

all-dressed

(*Quebec, New Brunswick, & Eastern Ontario*) designating an item of food (especially pizza or a hot dog) served with all the optional garnishes.

berry sugar

very fine granulated white sugar.

lassie / lassy

(*Newfoundland*) *informal* molasses.

maple butter

1 a spread made by heating maple syrup, then rapidly cooling it while stirring until it has a creamy consistency. **2** butter blended with maple syrup or maple sugar.

Sweets

bangbelly

(*Newfoundland*) a dense cake made of cooked rice, flour, molasses, raisins, salt pork, and spices.

blueberry buckle

(*Maritimes*) a cake topped with blueberries and a crumbly topping.

blueberry grunt

(*Maritimes*) a dessert of blueberries cooked in a saucepan with a dumpling-like topping.

bumbleberry

a mixture of berries, e.g. blackberries, raspberries, blueberries, strawberries, etc., sometimes also containing apples and rhubarb, used especially as a pie filling but also in jams, yogourt, etc. ❑ **Origin**: English dialect "bumble" = "rosehip, blackberry", possibly deformation of "bramble".

butter tart

a tart with a filling of butter, eggs, brown sugar, and usually raisins.

Cape Breton pork pie

a date-filled tart with short pastry.

coady

(*Newfoundland*) a thick sweetened sauce, usually made from boiled molasses.

dainties

(*Prairies & Northwestern Ontario*) fancy cookies, cakes, etc. usually served at social gatherings.

date squares

a dessert consisting of date filling spread on an oatmeal base and covered with a crumble topping, served cut into squares or rectangles.

figgy duff

(*Newfoundland*) a type of boiled pudding containing raisins. ❑ **Origin**: "fig" in some English dialects was used to mean "raisin"; "duff", which was a northern English form of "dough", means "pudding" in some dialects of English.

frankum

(*Newfoundland*) the hardened resin of a spruce tree, often used as chewing gum. ❏ **Origin**: shortening of *fran(c)kumsence*, 16th–17th century variant of "frankincense", used to mean "spruce or fir resin".

Indian ice cream

(*BC*) a dessert or drink made from whipped soapberries, sugar, and water.

matrimonial cake

(*Prairies*) date squares.

Nanaimo bars

a dessert consisting of a crust of chocolate and cookie crumbs, usually also including coconut and nuts, covered with a usually vanilla buttercream filling and a chocolate glaze, served cut into squares.

> It has not been determined why these are called Nanaimo bars. Ironically, the first evidence we have been able to find of the word is from a 1956 United Church cookbook from Humboldt, Saskatchewan.

oatcake

(*Nova Scotia*) a large dense oatmeal cookie.

peppermint knob

(*Newfoundland*) a hard, usually spherical, peppermint candy.

sugar pie

(*Quebec*) an open-faced or lattice-topped pie with a filling of brown or maple sugar mixed with cream and baked.

taffy

a chewy confection made by pouring hot maple syrup onto packed snow.

vinarterta

an Icelandic dessert consisting of several layers of white cake with a prune filling. ❑ **Pronunciation**: "VEENA tairta".

Doughnuts

Beaver Tail

proprietary a flat oval of deep-fried dough served with various garnishes, especially sugar and cinnamon.

bismarck

1 (*Alberta & Saskatchewan*) a sugar-coated jam-filled doughnut. **2** (*Manitoba*) a cream-filled doughnut, often with a chocolate glaze.

Burlington bun

(*Nova Scotia*) a sugar-coated jam-filled doughnut.

Dutchie

a usually square, raised, glazed doughnut containing raisins.

jambuster

(*Manitoba & Northwestern Ontario*) a sugar-coated jam-filled doughnut.

Persian

(*Northwestern Ontario*) an oblong doughnut covered with pink or white icing.

touton

(*Newfoundland*) a deep-fried flat round of bread dough, eaten with molasses. ❏ **Pronunciation**: TOUT'n.

Cheese

Cheezies

proprietary a snack food consisting of finger-sized pieces of extruded corn meal coated with powdered cheese.

Ermite

a creamy, semi-soft, and salty blue-veined cheese made in Quebec. ❏ **Pronunciation**: "air MEET". **Origin**: French *ermite* "hermit".

friulano

a mild, pale yellow, firm cow's milk cheese of a kind made originally in Friuli, northeastern Italy. ❏ **Pronunciation**: "free oo LAN oh".

nippy

informal (of food, especially cheese) piquant, sharp.

Oka

a variety of semi-soft cured cheese originally made by Trappist monks. ❏ **Origin**: named for Oka, Quebec, site of a Trappist monastery.

old

(of cheddar) aged 10–24 months.

In the US, aged cheese is referred to as "sharp". Many anecdotes are told of recent arrivals from the US thinking that "Old Fort" is a Canadian brand of cheddar, not realizing that "Old" is a descriptive term and "Fort" its French translation.

Preserves

gem jar

a Mason jar with a 78 mm diameter mouth.

preserves

food that has been home-preserved in jars; jams, jellies, pickles, canned fruits and vegetables, etc.

sealer

(especially *Prairies* & *BC*) a glass jar used for preserves etc., having a glass or metal lid secured by a metal band screwed onto the mouth of the jar.

sealer ring

(especially *Prairies* & *BC*) a rubber ring inserted between the lid and the rim of a sealer jar to ensure an airtight seal.

Where to Go When You Run Out of Food

CANEX

a store for military personnel on a Canadian military base.
❑ **Origin**: acronym from "Canadian Forces" + "Exchange".

dairy

(*Cape Breton*) a convenience store.

depanneur / dep

(*Quebec*) a convenience store.

Pronounced "deppa NURR". Canadian French, from French *dépanner*, from *panne* "breakdown, power failure". In European French, a *dépanneur* is a mechanic who fixes cars; the sense of "convenience store" is unique to Quebec French.

jug milk

(*Ontario*) a convenience store, especially one at which milk may be bought in returnable plastic jugs.

milk store

a convenience store.

tuck shop

a small store within a hospital, hotel, apartment block, etc., selling snacks and daily necessities to residents or guests.

Other Places to Grab a Bite

caf

informal a cafeteria.

casse-croûte

(*Quebec*) a snack bar. ❏ **Pronunciation**: "kass KROOT". **Origin**: Canadian French from French *casse-croûte* "snack", literally "break crust (of bread)".

Chinese café

(*Prairies*) a café in a small town, operated by a Chinese proprietor and serving Chinese and other food.

chip wagon

a mobile roadside stand or vehicle selling french fries and sometimes other fast foods.

sugar shack / cabane à sucre

(*Quebec*) a usually small establishment in a sugar bush serving dishes topped or flavoured with maple syrup and other traditional fare.

DRINKING AND CAROUSING

Drink Canada dry!

Canadians are not all the beer-swilling louts portrayed by the McKenzie brothers, but our predilection for beer and other alcoholic beverages has left its mark on the language. In no other country would the members of an otherwise sedate church choir be exhorted to use their "Molson muscles" when singing Palestrina (being a member of said choir, I can attest that of course none of us have beer bellies, so we understood this as just the choir director's inventive way of referring to our diaphragms!). Other countries may have ice cream parlours and pizza parlours, but only Canada has beer parlours, a rather prim-sounding name, when you think of it.

Some kinds of alcoholic drinks are associated with certain parts of the country. In Quebec, you can drink caribou, a mixture of red wine and whisky blanc (a colourless liquor distilled from cereal grains). In Newfoundland you can of course consume the famous screech , a potent dark rum, or, if you're feeling brave, some callibogus, a concoction of spruce beer, rum, and molasses. If you're in the Prairies, you can order a "red-eye", a beer and tomato juice combination.

On a somewhat more genteel front, cocktails that only a Canadian bartender would recognize are the Caesar or bloody Caesar and the brown cow. The wine made from grapes frozen on the vine that Canadians call "icewine" is called by its German name "Eiswein" if it comes from Europe. There is a kind of California icewine, but needless to say, they have to use freezers to freeze the grapes.

Of course, the law and society do not look kindly on all forms of alcohol consumption. Illegal after-hours drinking establishments have given Canadian English the word "booze can", and the derelicts reduced to drinking rubbing alcohol are known as "rubbies". Those guilty of drinking and driving are charged with the uniquely Canadian offence of "impaired" driving.

But lest you think that non-alcoholic beverages have failed to have an impact on Canadian English, you can ponder the iconic "double-double", a word much associated with the Tim Hortons doughnut store chain but used in coffee shops throughout the land. Anyone for a shot of screech in their double-double? Make it a two-ounce shot and I guess it would be a double-double double!

Beer

barley sandwich
  slang a beer.

beer parlour

a room in a hotel or tavern where beer is served.

beer slinger

informal a bartender.

beverage room

a lounge, bar, etc. where alcoholic drinks are sold.

flat

(especially *West*) a cardboard tray holding 24 cans of beer.

Molson muscle

slang a beer belly. ❏ **Origin**: Molson, a popular brand of beer.

red-eye

a drink made with tomato juice and beer.

stubby

informal a small squat bottle of beer with a short neck. (Also used in Australia.)

two-four

informal a case of twenty-four bottles of beer.

Other Drinks

alcool

(especially *Quebec*) a colourless, unflavoured alcoholic spirit distilled from cereal grains.

brown cow

a cocktail of coffee liqueur and milk or cream.

(Bloody) Caesar

a drink composed of vodka and tomato clam cocktail, usually garnished with celery.

callibogus

(especially *Newfoundland*) a beverage made from spruce beer and rum mixed with molasses.

caribou

(especially *Quebec*) a beverage made from red wine and whisky blanc.

icewine

a very sweet wine made from ripe grapes left to freeze on the vine before being picked, and still frozen when they go into the press.

L'Acadie Blanc

1 a hybrid wine grape grown in Nova Scotia. 2 a white wine made from this.

moose milk

1 a drink including alcoholic liquor (usually rum), milk, and often other ingredients, especially eggs. 2 home-distilled liquor. 3 any alcoholic drink.

rye

1 whisky blended from rye and other grains. 2 whisky distilled from fermented rye.

screech

a potent dark rum of Newfoundland. ❏ **Origin**: ultimately from Scottish dialect *screigh* "whisky".

swish

(*Atlantic Canada*) liquor made by filling a recently emptied rum barrel with boiling water and rotating it every few days for a couple of weeks.

VQA

the Vintners Quality Alliance, a body of winemakers, wine merchants, and federal government officials, whose initials are used to designate a Canadian wine certified as meeting certain standards of taste and conforming to statutory regulations.

whisky blanc

(*Quebec*) a type of colourless whisky made from distilled grain alcohol.

How much is too much?

forty-pounder

slang a forty-ounce bottle of liquor.

mickey

a small bottle of liquor, usually 375 ml.

pint

(*Maritimes*) a mickey of liquor.

Texas mickey

informal a 130-ounce bottle of alcohol, especially rye whisky.

twenty-six

a 26-ounce bottle of liquor.

Places to Drink

booze can
an illegal bar, especially one operating in a private home.

brasserie
(*Quebec*) a pub. ❑ **Origin**: French, = "brewery".

off-sale
(*BC, Alberta, & North*) **1** the sale of liquor for consumption elsewhere than at the place of sale. **2** an alcoholic drink sold for consumption elsewhere.

For the teetotaller

double-double
a cup of coffee with a double serving of both sugar and cream.

drinking box
a small plasticized cardboard carton of juice etc. packaged with a straw that can be inserted through a foil-covered hole in the top.

Freshie
proprietary dated a fruit-flavoured powder mixed with water and sugar to make a drink.

Labrador tea
an infusion made from the leathery evergreen leaves of a shrub of the heath family.

soopollalie

(*BC*) a thick drink made from crushed buffalo berries.
❑ **Origin**: from *soop*, variant of "soap" + Chinook Jargon
olallie "berry".

switchel

(*Newfoundland*) *historical* weak tea without milk and sweetened with molasses, drunk especially by fishermen and sealers
at sea. ❑ **Origin**: possibly related to "swizzle" (also of uncertain origin); applied earlier to a drink of water and molasses.

syrup

(*Newfoundland*) a fruit-flavoured drink of water and syrup; a
cordial.

Vi-Co

(*Saskatchewan*) *proprietary* chocolate milk.

FOR THE
LOVE
OF THE
GAME

THE GOOD OLE HOCKEY GAME

Hockey Words in Canada

A good way to test if your dictionary is truly Canadian is to see whether its first definition of "hockey" is "a game played on ice" or "a game played on a field"! The game that has such an unshakeable hold on the national psyche has also made its mark on Canadian English.

Pay a visit to any "ice palace" (as only a Canadian would call an arena), and you'll see "pucksters" stickhandling their way through some tricky manoeuvres. "Dekes", deceptive moves that draw the defence player out of position. The "spinarama", a word invented by Danny Gallivan, the long-time play-by-play announcer for Montreal Canadiens' games, to describe a manoeuvre perfected by the Montreal defenceman Serge Savard.

When barely out of diapers, Canadian kids are organized into the hierarchy of minor hockey, with distinctly Canadian names for each level. A new Canadian might be mystified by "atoms" that are not molecular particles, "mosquitoes" that are not biting insects, "midgets" who aren't any shorter than normal, and the mysterious biological transformation that turns a mosquito into a bantam (not a chicken!).

All of these young Gretzkys are overseen by that Canadian institution, the hockey mom, who chauffeurs them to practices at ungodly hours, cheers them on at games, and sometimes is prone to "hockey rage". Hockey moms are not of course to be confused with the other females who frequent hockey rinks, the notorious "puck bunnies" (young women who chase after hockey players).

Canadians even have an affectionate name for hockey (especially informal hockey): "shinny", a word that has been with us since the 1840s and is a variant of "shinty", a game like field hockey played in Scotland. In 1867, there were reports of young lads in Kingston amusing themselves by tripping young ladies on the public skating rink with their shinty sticks. Some things never change!

Fancy stickhandling, ragging the puck, crucial faceoffs, and even the occasional spinarama move, not to mention dropping the gloves when things get unpleasant and hanging up one's skates when it's over—in Canada, the political arena is as likely a venue for these activities as the hockey arena, thanks to our predilection for using hockey vocabulary metaphorically. Consider these journalistic descriptions of some politicians not usually renowned for their athletic prowess:

"It won't be long until David Tsubouchi can rag the puck for the entire question period without saying a word."

"When you think about it, Mr. Klein's entire governmental agenda is based on the spinarama."

"Joe Clark must now stickhandle route to new federalism."

"Joe Ghiz hangs up his skates because he is feeling too old and tired for the game of politics."

The hockey mom, however, is yet to show up in the political arena. Perhaps it's because the Speaker of the House doesn't take kindly to people shouting, "Hey ref, are you BLIND???" from the Visitors'

Gallery! Whether there is a parliamentary equivalent of the puck bunny I will leave to those who spend more time in Ottawa than I do.

ball hockey

1 a version of hockey played in a gymnasium or in an arena without ice, using a hard plastic ball in place of a puck. 2 a version of hockey, usually without formal rules, played on a paved surface, using a tennis ball instead of a puck.

dipsy-doodle

slang evade the defending team by using feints, dekes, swerving motions, and finesse in stickhandling etc.

foot hockey

(*Ontario*) a schoolyard game resembling soccer but using a puck-sized ball (e.g. a tennis ball) and hockey-sized goals, usually played on a paved surface.

hockey cushion

a skating rink with hockey boards, especially an outdoor rink of natural ice.

ice pad

a rink of natural or artificial ice for skating, playing hockey, curling, etc.

ice palace

informal a hockey arena.

pond hockey

1 informal or disorganized hockey played on a frozen pond. 2 hockey played with seemingly little attention to discipline, defensive strategy, etc.

puckster

slang a hockey player.

road apple

slang historical a frozen piece of horse manure used as a hockey puck, especially on the Prairies.

schlockey

a children's game played on a four-foot by eight-foot framed plywood sheet stationed between two players, in which each player, using a cut-off hockey stick, attempts to score by shooting a puck past a centre barrier and through a hole in the framing board at the opposing end. ❑ **Origin**: punningly after "hockey" + "schlocky".

shinny

1 informal pickup hockey played usually without nets, referees, or equipment except for skates, sticks, and a ball or puck or an object serving as a puck. **2** street hockey. **3** *informal* hockey. ❑ **Origin**: a variant of "shinty", a game similar to field hockey originally played in Scotland.

spinarama

an evasive move consisting of an abrupt 360-degree turn.

sponge hockey

a form of hockey played on ice with rubber-soled boots and a sponge puck.

sponge puck

a hockey puck made of hard sponge, used in recreational play or with young children.

street hockey / road hockey

a version of hockey played on a street usually by children using hockey sticks and a ball in place of a puck.

SKATING

barrel-jumping

a sport in which a skater jumps over a row of barrels lying on their sides.

bobskate

a child's skate consisting of two parallel blades which are attached with straps to a shoe or boot.

carnival

a non-competitive performance given by the members of a figure skating club.

cheese cutter

(*Quebec & Eastern Ontario*) a bobskate.

power skating

a skating technique aiming to increase a skater's power, speed, and agility by the most efficient use of the skate blades and of the muscles and alignment of the body.

skate-a-thon

a prolonged period of skating, organized to raise money for a charity or cause.

tube skate

an ice skate with the blade running along a hollow metal tube.

CURLING

Brier
the bonspiel for the Canadian men's national curling championship. ❑ **Origin**: the name of the trophy, originally sponsored by the Macdonald tobacco company, which sold a brand of tobacco called "Brier", the brier plant root being used to make pipes.

carspiel
a bonspiel in which curlers compete for a car or cars.

cashspiel
a bonspiel in which curlers compete for cash prizes.

jam-pail curling
(*Prairies*) a form of curling in which the rocks are replaced by ice-filled four-pound jam tins, with a bent steel rod serving as a handle.

playdown
a playoff match in a tournament etc.

BASEBALL

backcatcher
the fielder positioned behind home plate in baseball.

fastball
a variety of the game of softball, featuring fast underhand pitching.

sno-pitch / snow pitch

a game similar to slo-pitch, played on snow.

three-pitch

a variety of softball in which the batter cannot draw a walk, having only three chances to hit a ball delivered underhand by a teammate.

FOOTBALL

---

convert

the scoring of points after a touchdown by kicking the ball between the uprights (for one additional point) or by carrying or passing the ball over the defending team's goal line (for two additional points).

designated import

(formerly) an import player who may enter the game at a position, when the total allowable number of import players is already in the game.

homebrew

a person, especially a sports competitor, who is a native of the country or locality where the competition is held.

import

a professional player who learned to play football outside of Canada (usually in the US) before the age of seventeen, or who started to learn football after the age of seventeen outside Canada.

major

informal a touchdown.

non-import

a player who trained only in Canada or who lived in Canada for five years before the age of fifteen.

rouge / single point

a single point scored when the receiving team fails to run a kick out of the end zone, such as on a punt, kickoff, or missed field goal.

safety / safety touch

1 a play in which the offensive team moves the ball into its own end zone and either downs the ball or is tackled there or moves it out of bounds, resulting in two points being awarded to the defensive team. **2** the two points so awarded.

NOT QUITE THE BIG LEAGUES

atom

a level of children's sports, usually involving children aged 9 to 11.

bantam

a level of amateur sport, usually involving children aged 13 to 15.

carded

(of an amateur athlete) receiving government funding to pursue training.

espoir

a junior elite athlete potentially of national team calibre.

house league

1 a sports league in which the players on all teams are members of the same school, organization, etc. **2** a league in children's sports in which any child may play without having to pass a tryout.

industrial league

informal a sports league, especially in hockey, of teams sponsored by corporations.

juvenile

(of a sports team, league, player, etc.) involving teenagers, especially between the ages of 15 and 19.

major junior

the highest level of junior amateur hockey competition.

midget

a level of amateur sport, usually involving players aged 16 to 17.

minor league

an amateur league for children and youth, especially in hockey, football, etc.

mosquito

an initiation level of sports competition for young children.

novice

a level of children's sports, usually involving children aged 8 to 9.

peewee

    a level of amateur sport, usually involving children aged 12 to 13.

rep league

    a league in children's sports for players with stronger abilities, organized on a more competitive footing than house leagues, and requiring players to pass tryouts.

tyke

    an initiation level of sports competition for young children.

OTHER WAYS TO STAY IN SHAPE

baggataway

    a forerunner of lacrosse played by the Aboriginal peoples of eastern North America, in which opposing teams attempt to propel a ball into the other's goal using a net attached to a curved stick. ❑ **Pronunciation**: "buh GATTA way". **Origin**: Ojibwa *paka'atowe* "he plays lacrosse".

box lacrosse / boxla

    a form of lacrosse played in an enclosed area (usually a hockey rink without ice) by teams of six players.

carpet bowling

    an indoor game similar to lawn bowling, played with either round balls or asymmetrical bowls.

five-pin bowling

    a variety of bowling in which players have three chances to knock down five pins, each of different scoring value, using a smaller ball than in 10-pin bowling.

inter-lacrosse

a coeducational, non-contact version of lacrosse played indoors or outdoors with a moulded plastic stick and a soft, air-filled ball, and involving continuous running. ❑ **Origin**: from "inter-" designating at once French *intérieur* "indoor", "international", and "between", inter-lacrosse providing an opportunity to play lacrosse in the winter, between box lacrosse seasons.

mini-putt

miniature golf.

ringette

a game resembling hockey, played (especially by women and girls) on ice with a straight stick and a rubber ring.

scrub

an informal match played by children, amateurs, etc.; a pickup game.

Wen-Do

proprietary a program of self-defence designed for women, which emphasizes awareness and avoidance of potentially dangerous situations as well as appropriate reactions, including, as a last resort, physical attacks directed against the particularly vulnerable areas of an assailant's body. ❑ **Origin**: literally "women's way", from Anglo-Saxon *cwēne* "woman" + Japanese *dō* "way".

IN OUR FREE TIME

Places to Socialize
🍁 *Fun CanSpeak Facts:* Let's Party! 🍁

X-Rated: Sex, Drugs, and Gambling

Canadians Just Wanna Have Fun

Take the Day (or Week) Off

Arts and Entertainment

Keeping in Touch

Let's Party!

Are Canadians party animals? We certainly have our fair share of party-related words.

Weddings, of course, top the list when it comes to big bashes, and there are many Canadian social events associated with them. A Canadian wedding tradition that has mostly become obsolete is the "trousseau tea", a party hosted by a bride's mother for neighbours and acquaintances (usually those who didn't make it onto the actual wedding guest list), at which shower and wedding gifts, the bride's trousseau, the contents of her hope chest, and so forth, were displayed.

But some uniquely Canadian wedding traditions are still alive and well. Anyone who has lived in Manitoba is familiar with the "social", a public dance held in honour of a couple about to be married, with proceeds from sales of tickets and liquor given to the couple to help them start out on their new life. This phenomenon is known in rural Ontario as a "buck and doe" or "stag and doe", and, astoundingly to British speakers for whom the word means something else entirely, a "shag" in Thunder Bay.

A fixture of most of the socials and wedding receptions I attended in my youth in Manitoba was a Ukrainian dance called the "butterfly", in which trios of dancers alternate between promenading slowly around the dance floor and whirling each other around in circles. Another Prairie wedding tradition is the "presentation", meaning the custom of giving money as a wedding gift. If your wedding invitation says "presentation only", don't come bearing a Corningware casserole!

Graduations are another big milestone marked by parties, and the use of the word "grad" to mean a dinner dance celebrating graduation is unique to Canada. It was a surprise to me, when I moved to southern Ontario, to hear people use the word "prom", which I had always thought was uniquely American.

It is highly unlikely that anyone would use the word "whoop-up" to describe anything as sedate and genteel as a trousseau tea, but some of the rowdier socials might qualify for this designation, which seems to be more common in Alberta than elsewhere in Canada. This is not surprising, considering that the notorious Fort Whoop-Up, a fort of the "whisky traders" (Americans who illegally sold rotgut to the Indians north of the 49th parallel in the 1870s), was located in what is now Southern Alberta.

Another kind of wingding that tends to get rowdy is the "bush party" or "field party", at which a group of (usually young) people stand around in a woodlot or field and consume large amounts of beer.

Even though they may not use the word, Maritimers have their own kind of whoop-ups. A kitchen party or kitchen racket is an informal entertainment held in a person's home, at which participants play music, sing, dance, or tell stories. A soiree in Newfoundland is a large party with singing, dancing, and eating. Another Newfoundland social event is the "screech-in", a jocular ceremony where "come-from-aways" are initiated to honorary Newfoundland citizenship by being made to drink screech, dip their toe in the cold ocean, and kiss a cod.

From trousseau teas to screech-ins, Canadians clearly know how to have a good time.

Your Place or Mine

bush party
a usually large social gathering, especially of young people, held in a woodlot or bush etc., and usually with the object of consuming beer.

coffee row
(*Saskatchewan*) a regular gathering of people for coffee and gossip at a café etc., especially in a rural area.

come-and-go
(*Saskatchewan*) a reception or party during which guests are invited to drop in to a person's home; an open house.

community hall
a hall maintained by a community for holding suppers, dances, wedding receptions, etc.

field party
a large outdoor party held in an open field, usually with the object of consuming beer.

fowl supper / fall supper
a fundraising dinner at which turkey or other fowl is served, held in the autumn by a church or community group.

grad
informal **1** a graduation ceremony; commencement. **2** a dinner dance to celebrate graduation; a prom.

kitchen party / kitchen racket

Atlantic Canada an informal entertainment held in a person's home, at which participants play music, sing, dance, etc.

levee

a New Year's Day reception held by the Governor General or by a Lieutenant-Governor, or by a mayor, bishop, etc.

lobster supper

(*Maritimes*) a meal, usually served in a community hall, featuring boiled lobster served with melted butter and accompanied by copious salads, bread rolls, clam chowder, and cake or pie.

mechoui

(*Quebec*) a meal of meat, especially lamb or mutton, roasted on a spit over a fire. ❑ **Pronunciation:** "MAY shwee". **Origin:** French from North African Arabic *mashwi*, "grilled foods".

milling frolic

(*Nova Scotia*) **1** *historical* a gathering at which participants pound new wool to raise the nap, usually with singing, dancing, etc. **2** a cultural event at which songs traditionally sung at these are performed.

scoff

informal (*Atlantic Canada*) a big meal, especially of seafood, served in conjunction with a party.

soiree

(*Newfoundland*) **1** a social gathering held by an organization or service club. **2** a large party or community social with singing, dancing, and eating. ❑ **Pronunciation:** "swar EE".

time

(*Atlantic Canada*) a festive gathering of friends and relatives, especially in celebration of an event, such as a wedding, or community event.

tintamarre

a noisy parade, especially the annual celebration on National Acadian Day, August 15, involving a procession, the banging of pots and pans, playing of musical instruments, etc. ❑ **Pronunciation:** "tanta MAR". **Origin**: French, ="din".

whoop-up

informal a noisy celebration or party.

Weddings

presentation

(*Prairies*) **1** a wedding at which the bride and groom receive gifts of money rather than things. **2** a gift of money at such a wedding.

shag

(*Northwestern Ontario*) a stag and doe party. ❑ **Origin**: blend of "shower" + "stag.

social

(*Prairies*) a public social gathering held before a wedding to raise money for the couple that is to be married.

stag and doe / buck and doe

(*Ontario*) a dance held in honour of an engaged couple, to whom the money raised from ticket sales is given.

stagette

an all-female celebration in honour of a woman about to marry.

trousseau tea

dated a party hosted by a bride's mother for neighbours and acquaintances, at which shower and wedding gifts, the bride's trousseau, contents of her hope chest, etc. are displayed.

X-RATED: SEX, DRUGS, AND GAMBLING

In Flagrante Delicto

body-rub parlour

an establishment at which body rubs and often other sexual services are provided.

(common) bawdy house

a brothel.

doob

slang (*West*) a condom.

found-in

a person arrested for being discovered in a bawdy house or an illegal bar or gambling establishment.

French safe

slang a condom.

living off the avails

benefiting from the proceeds or profits of another person's, especially a prostitute's, labour.

Marijuana

BC Bud
informal high-potency marijuana grown in BC, with a tetra-hydrocannabinol content of 15% to 25%. ❑ **Origin**: abbreviation of "British Columbia" + "bud", the buds of the cannabis plant being the richest source of THC.

compassion club
a non-profit organization which sells marijuana for medical use.

grow op / grow
informal an illegal marijuana-growing operation, usually in someone's home.

Quebec gold
informal high-potency marijuana grown in Quebec.

smoke up
smoke a drug, especially marijuana.

Betting

barbotte
(especially *Quebec*) a gambling game similar to craps but played with three dice.

exactor
a bet on the first- and second-place finishers in a race, specifying their order of finish. ❑ **Origin**: alteration of "exacta", from Latin American Spanish *quiniela exacta* "exact quinella".

50/50 draw
a fundraiser in which participants buy tickets, with the winner taking half of the total take, and the other half going to the charity etc.

Nevada ticket
a lottery ticket on which perforated paper strips are torn away to reveal a series of images which, if matching, constitute a win.

triactor
a bet on the first three finishers in a horse race, specifying their order of finish. ❑ **Origin**: blend of "tri-" + "exactor".

CANADIANS JUST WANNA HAVE FUN

Games and Other Distractions

bathtub race
an event in which bathtubs are motorized and piloted across bodies of water.

blanket toss
an Inuit game in which a large circle of animal skin or canvas held around the edges by several people is used to toss a person in the air.

bumper shining
(*Manitoba* & *Saskatchewan*) the practice, engaged in by children, of holding on to a car's rear bumper on a snowy or icy road so as to be dragged along for a ride.

burbee

(in east end Toronto) wall ball, a variety of baseball played in a schoolyard by two or more players, in which the batter's strike zone is represented by a box drawn on a wall, and singles, doubles, triples, and home runs are achieved by hitting a tennis ball past certain designated landmarks.

Chinese skipping

(*West*) a form of skipping in which a circle of elastic is looped around the ankles of two participants then moved progressively higher while the other participants attempt various jumping manoeuvres.

crokinole

a game in which wooden discs are flicked across a round wooden board towards its centre. ❏ **Origin:** French *croquignole* "a flip, flick".

Halloween apples!

(*Prairies*) uttered by children going door to door on Halloween to collect candies etc.

high kick

a traditional Inuit game in which participants attempt to kick an object suspended above them and land on the foot used to kick with.

jumpsies

(*Ontario*) a form of skipping in which a circle of elastic is looped around the ankles of two participants then moved progressively higher while the other participants attempt various jumping manoeuvres.

knock on ginger / knock down ginger / knock-a-door ginger

(*Prairies*) a children's game involving knocking on a door or ringing a doorbell and running away before the door is answered.

murderball

a game in which players in opposing teams attempt to hit their opponents with a large, inflated ball.

nicky nicky nine doors

a children's game involving knocking on a door or ringing a doorbell and running away before the door is answered.

In the cards

kaiser

(*Saskatchewan*) a whist-based card game played especially in Saskatchewan.

poker derby

(*Manitoba, Saskatchewan, & Northwestern Ontario*) a competition in which participants race to a series of points (usually over a large area) collecting a single playing card at each one, the winner being determined by a combination of time taken and the poker hand collected; a poker run.

tarabish

(*Cape Breton*) a card game based on bridge. ❑ **Pronunciation:** "TAR bish".

Toys

Jolly Jumper

proprietary an infant swing which suspends a baby in a harness in a standing position just above the floor, allowing the child to jump, exercise its legs, etc.

Ookpik

a doll resembling an owl, originally handcrafted of sealskin by Inuit artisans, now mass-produced and sold as a souvenir. ❑ **Origin:** Inuktitut *ukpik* "snowy owl".

tea doll

(among the Innu of Labrador) a rag doll designed to be packed with two or three pounds of tea, thus serving as a means of transporting tea in the bush as well as a child's toy.

TAKE THE DAY (OR WEEK) OFF

Holidays

(Alberta) Family Day

the third Monday in February, a holiday in Alberta.

BC Day

the name of the August civic holiday in British Columbia.

Boxing Week

the week between Christmas and New Year's Day.

Canada Day

the annual holiday commemorating the creation of the Dominion of Canada (then New Brunswick, Nova Scotia, Quebec, and Ontario) on 1 July 1867.

civic holiday

a holiday that is commonly observed but not legislated, especially the first Monday in August, observed as a holiday in all of Canada except Quebec and PEI.

construction holiday

(*Quebec*) a holiday traditionally taken by construction workers in Quebec during the last two weeks of July, often taken as a holiday by many other Quebecers as well.

Discovery Day

1 (in the Yukon) a statutory holiday observed on the third Monday in August, commemorating the discovery of gold in the Klondike on August 17, 1896. **2** (in Newfoundland prior to 1993) a statutory holiday observed on the Monday nearest June 24, the date on which John Cabot landed in Newfoundland in 1497.

Dominion Day

historical the former name for Canada Day.

Fête nationale

(in Quebec) the official name for the holiday celebrated on June 24, formerly (and commonly still) called St. Jean Baptiste Day.

Flag Day

15 February, the anniversary of the adoption of the Maple Leaf flag in 1965.

Heritage Day

1 the third Monday in February, marked unofficially as a celebration of Canada's history and heritage. **2** (in the Yukon) the fourth Friday in February, observed as a holiday in the public service and some other workplaces. **3** a day designated by a particular region, ethnic group, etc. as a time to celebrate a shared history and culture.

May Two-Four

informal Victoria Day.

Named punningly after May 24th, the official date of the holiday, and after "two-four", in reference to copious consumption of beer over the holiday.

Memorial Day

(*Newfoundland*) a statutory holiday, 1 July, commemorating losses to the Newfoundland Regiment at the battle of the Somme.

Natal Day

(in Nova Scotia) a day celebrating the founding of a town or city, usually now observed on the first Monday in August.

National Acadian Day

August 15, on which Acadians celebrate their culture and heritage.

Nunavut Day

July 9, observed as a holiday in commemoration of the final signing of the Nunavut Land Claim on July 9, 1993.

Patriotes Day

(*Quebec*) the official name in Quebec from 2003 onwards for Victoria Day.

Queen's Birthday

in BC and Newfoundland and Labrador, a holiday falling on the Monday immediately preceding 25 May; Victoria Day.

Regatta Day

(*Newfoundland*) **1** a marine event held annually on usually the first Wednesday in August on Quidi Vidi Lake in St. John's, associated with a carnival that features bands, games, and other attractions. **2** a provincial statutory holiday held on this day.

Remembrance Day

November 11, the anniversary of the armistice at the end of the First World War, on which the war dead are commemorated.

Saint-Jean-Baptiste Day

(in Quebec) the former official name (still commonly in use) for the Fête nationale, June 24. ❑ **Origin**: French, literally "St. John the Baptist" (whose feast is celebrated on this day), patron saint of French Canadians.

Saskatchewan Day

a statutory holiday occurring on the first Monday in August.

Simcoe Day

(*Southern Ontario*) (especially in Toronto) a civic holiday celebrated on the first Monday in August.

statutory holiday / stat

a public holiday established by federal or provincial statute.

Thanksgiving

an annual holiday, originally for giving thanks to God for the success of the harvest, celebrated on the second Monday in October.

Victoria Day

a holiday falling on the Monday immediately preceding 25 May.

Things to Do on Holiday

exhibition / ex

a large regional fair, especially with amusements, agricultural exhibits, and craft displays, usually lasting for an extended period.

Stampede

an exhibition or fair involving rodeo events and other contests and entertainment.

ARTS AND ENTERTAINMENT

TV and Radio

ACTRA

Alliance of Canadian Cinema, Television and Radio Artists, a union for writers, performers, and broadcast journalists and researchers.

CanCon

informal Canadian content, especially with reference to regulated quotas in broadcasting.

CanCult

informal Canadian culture.

cultural sovereignty

the power of a country to maintain independence in its cultural activities from another, culturally dominant, nation.

hotline / open-line

a radio or television phone-in show.

hotliner

1 an on-air personality who runs a phone-in show. **2** a person who calls a phone-in show.

Mother Corp.

informal the CBC.

open-liner

the host of an open-line radio or television program.

téléroman

a French-language prime-time soap opera.

Singing and Dancing

ayaya

singing, typically among the Inuit, in which the sounds *ay-ay-a* are used rather than words.

butterfly

a social dance in which trios of people alternate between promenading slowly around the dance floor and whirling each other around in circles.

chin music

(*Newfoundland*) sung or hummed music as accompaniment to a dance.

drum dance

(among the Inuit) a dance, performed to an accompaniment of drumming, combining traditional Inuit dancing with Scottish and French-Canadian jigs and reels.

hamatsa

a dance among the Kwagiulth in which the main dancer is inspired by the spirit of a man-eating monster hungering for human flesh. ❑ **Origin**: Kwagiulth.

music man

(*Manitoba*) a disc jockey who plays recorded music at a dance etc.

Red River jig

1 a Metis step dance originating in the Red River Colony, combining French-Canadian dance rhythms and Aboriginal powwow steps, including an element of improvisation by dancers who compete for originality and precise footwork. **2** the music for this.

throat singing

(in Inuit culture) a type of singing, usually performed by two women face to face, uttering deep, rhythmic sounds evocative of animal and bird noises, sometimes with a competitive aspect.

Traditional Crafts

birchbark biting
a modern Aboriginal handicraft, made by biting designs into birch bark.

catalogne
(*Quebec*) a kind of weaving using rags as the weft and widely spaced threads as the warp. ❑ **Pronunciation**: "catta LONYA".

cotton batten
fluffy cotton wadding used for crafts, first aid, etc.

Economuseum
proprietary a small business which practises a traditional craft or skill (e.g. paper making, cheese making, apple growing, etc.) and also acts as a museum by allowing visitors to observe the work and learn more about its history through displays and other interpretive materials.

pysanka
a dyed Ukrainian Easter egg with elaborate and intricate designs inscribed using wax and a stylus. The plural is **pysanky**.

quillwork
art using porcupine quills to decorate clothing, teepees, and utilitarian items, done by a number of Aboriginal groups, especially the Mi'kmaq.

tufting

(in northern Canada) **1** a handicraft in which plucked moose-hair or caribou hair is dyed, gathered in tufts, stitched in patterns on a background of fabric or leather, and finally contoured or sculpted with clippers. **2** a product of such handiwork.

KEEPING IN TOUCH

coordinates

(*Quebec*) one's contact details, i.e. phone number, mailing address, email address, etc.

hasty note

a small folded card or sheet of paper with a decoration on the front and the rest left blank for writing short letters etc.

mobility

(especially in names of companies) mobile telecommunications systems, e.g. cellphones, pagers, etc.

moccasin telegraph

(especially *North*) *informal* **1** a means of transmitting rumours or unofficial information by word of mouth; the grapevine. **2** information so relayed.

PEACE, ORDER, AND GOOD GOVERNMENT

Politics and Government

✿ *Fun CanSpeak Facts:* A Leg to Stand On ✿

Law

A leg to stand on

Did you know that if someone phones you from the Ontario legislature, the call display function identifies your caller intriguingly as the "leg assembly"? Imagine if you weren't Canadian! You would be equally confused by references to the "leg library", or (apparently a common occurrence in Edmonton) by an invitation to have lunch on the "grounds of the leg". Not only is the shortened form "leg" (pronounced "ledge" to minimize confusion, though radio news reports "from the ledge" might be cause for some alarm) unique to Canadian English, but so are both "legislative building" and the use of "legislature" to mean the building itself as well as the legislative body seated there.

Other political terms used by Canadians might confuse you too. Isn't everyone supposed to have a "responsible government"? Why on earth would we put journalists in the lock-up just because the provincial budget is being announced? Are horses involved in riding associations (and is that why our official head of state is the "GG")?

Speaking of horses, who are the Horsemen? Is the "impaired driving lawyer" you see advertised on the sides of buses really someone you want to hire? For the law, too, has its unique Canadianisms. Did you know that you can charter a criminal as well as a plane in Canada? The very grammatical-sounding conditional sentence (not to be confused with a notwithstanding clause) is not a sentence starting with "If . . .", but, as a Crown prosecutor of my acquaintance described it, "when, instead of going to the Big House, the guilty bastard goes home, watches TV, and feels remorseful". And, for those criminals who do get a custodial sentence, there's the possibility of day release to attend school or for employment. The term "day release" in British English applies also to a system of allowing days off for education—but for employees, not prisoners. Prisoners, employees . . . come to think of it, it's not *that* different! And then there are those bad guys who are never let out: "Murderer declared dangerous offender," a newspaper headline screams. "Well, duh!" would be the non-Canadian's reaction.

Parliamentary Affairs

amending formula
a prescribed method for amending a constitution specifying the proportions of various interested parties that must assent for an amendment to be passed.

bear-pit session
a meeting, especially a political one, in which audience members question one or more representatives, leaders, candidates, etc.

bell-ringing
the ringing of bells in a legislative assembly to summon members for a vote, especially when provoked or prolonged by Opposition members as a tactic for stalling debate.

bring down
present a budget, law, report, etc. (Also used in Australia and New Zealand.)

cabinet order

an administrative order determined by the cabinet and formally issued by the sovereign or the sovereign's representative, usually to deal with routine matters or to establish detailed regulations concerning acts passed by Parliament; an order-in-council.

the Charter

the Canadian Charter of Rights and Freedoms.

consensus government

a form of government operating in the NWT and Nunavut, in which all the members of each territory's Legislative Assembly are elected as independent candidates rather than as members of political parties, the premier and cabinet are selected by secret-ballot voting in the legislature, and non-cabinet members serve as an unofficial opposition.

co-operative federalism

the policy or practice of the federal government consulting with provincial governments and making joint decisions on matters that are of shared or strictly federal jurisdiction.

die on the Order Paper

(of a bill) fail to be voted on before the end of a legislative session.

executive council

1 the members of a provincial or territorial cabinet. **2** *historical* (in colonial government) a body of advisers appointed by the governor.

executive federalism

the practice of establishing Canadian constitutional, social, and economic policy at meetings of first ministers and cabinet ministers, especially behind closed doors.

feds

slang the federal government.

file

issues and responsibilities in a specified area, considered collectively.

first minister

1 the prime minister of Canada. **2** the premier of a province.

Government Leader

the leader of any of the Territorial governments.

Green Chamber

the House of Commons or a provincial legislature, so called because of its green carpet and upholstery.

House of Assembly

(in Nova Scotia and Newfoundland and Labrador) the provincial legislature.

indemnity

the salary paid to a Member of Parliament or of a Legislative Assembly.

leg.

informal a legislature. ❑ **Pronunciation:** "ledge".

legislative building / legislature

the building in which a provincial legislative assembly meets.

lob (ball)

(especially in the House of Commons etc.) a question that is easy to answer, especially one that is made intentionally so in order to make the respondent look competent, articulate, etc.

lock-up

a type of press conference where members of the media are allowed to examine a government budget in a locked room before it is brought down in the legislature, but are not allowed to leave the room or file any reports until the budget is officially brought down.

National Assembly

the provincial legislature of Quebec.

non-confidence

a lack of majority support for a government, policy, etc. expressed by a legislature.

notwithstanding clause

Section 33 of the Canadian Charter of Rights and Freedoms, which allows Parliament and the provincial legislatures to override Charter clauses covering fundamental freedoms and legal and equality rights.

Parliament Hill / the Hill

1 the hill in Ottawa on which the Parliament Buildings stand.
2 the federal government of Canada.

patriate

bring (legislation, especially a constitution) under the authority of the autonomous country to which it applies, used with reference to laws passed on behalf of that country by its former mother country.

premier

the head of government of a province or territory.

Privy Council Office

an administrative body which coordinates the activities of the federal Cabinet, provides advice to the prime minister, deputy prime minister, and government house leaders, and implements government objectives.

provincehood

the quality or status of being a province.

Province House

the name of the legislative building in Nova Scotia and Prince Edward Island.

provincialization

the transfer of responsibilities etc. to the provincial level.

Queen's Park

1 the grounds and building in Toronto where the Ontario legislature is situated. **2** the government of Ontario.

Queen's Printer

an official printer of bills and reports, office stationery, bulletins, etc. for the federal or provincial governments.

question period

a period of time set aside each day during parliamentary proceedings in which members may question government ministers.

Red Chamber

the Senate chamber of the Parliament Buildings in Ottawa, so called because of its red carpet and draperies.

redistribution

the reapportioning, made every ten years, of the number of seats in the House of Commons to reflect changes in the size of the population.

reeve

(in Ontario and the Western provinces) the elected leader of the council of a town or other rural municipality.

registry office

a government office where private property, such as vehicles, real estate, etc., may be registered and where records of ownership are kept.

representation by population / rep by pop

1 the concept that legislative representation should be based proportionally on population rather than on a method giving equal representation to different regions in spite of population differences. **2** *historical* such representation in the Province of Canada after 1851, in opposition to representation divided equally between Canada East and Canada West.

responsible government

a form of government in which the cabinet or executive branch is held collectively responsible and accountable to an elected legislature, and may remain in power only so long as it has the support of the legislature.

saw-off

1 an arrangement between political rivals in which each agrees not to contest a seat etc. held by the other. **2** any compromise involving mutual concessions. **3** a tie, deadlock, stalemate, etc.

scrum

1 a situation where a crowd of reporters surround and interrogate a politician in an impromptu, informal, or disorderly manner. **2** the crowd of reporters in such a situation.

Speech from the Throne / Throne Speech

a statement summarizing the government's proposed measures, read by the sovereign, Governor General, or Lieutenant-Governor at the opening of a session of Parliament or a legislature.

Treasury Board

a committee of the Privy Council responsible for reviewing and prioritizing planned government expenditures and programs etc.

Triple-E Senate

a proposed senate that would have more effective powers than the existing Senate and which would consist of elected members equally representing the provinces, as introduced and advocated by Alberta premier Don Getty in the late 1980s. ❏ **Origin**: from the three *E*'s of Equal, Elected, and Effective.

vote of non-confidence

a vote indicating that the majority does not support a policy of the governing party, as a result of which the governing party is usually forced to resign.

Political Nicknames

Big Blue Machine

the Ontario Progressive Conservative Party during the premiership of William Davis (1971–85).

Bloquiste

a member of the Bloc Québécois.

Créditiste

historical a member or supporter of the Quebec wing of the Social Credit Party.

felquiste

historical a member of the FLQ (Front de Libération du Québec), a Quebec separatist terrorist organization especially active in the 1960s and early 1970s.

Grit

a supporter or member of the Liberal Party.

The term was originally used to designate a supporter of the Clear Grit Party, a liberal reform party in Upper Canada during the 1840s and 1850s, which formed the basis of the Liberal Party after Confederation.

Péquiste

a supporter or member of the Parti Québécois.

Red Tory

a member of a Conservative party who holds more liberal views on certain (especially social) issues than his or her fellow party members.

Rhino

a member of the Rhinoceros Party, a spoof political party which first ran candidates in the 1960s; the party's goal is to demonstrate the supposed shortcomings of the traditional Canadian political parties.

Socred

a member of the Social Credit Party.

Trudeaumania

widespread popularity of, and fascination with, Pierre Elliott Trudeau among the Canadian public, especially during the election campaign of 1968.

Getting and Spending

download

shift or relegate responsibilities or costs for (a program) from one level of government to a lower one.

equalization payment / equalization grant

an unconditional transfer by the federal government of funds from general revenues to a poorer province to ensure that all provincial governments provide comparable levels of service and taxation.

have-not province

a province whose per capita tax revenue falls below a certain average level and which is therefore entitled to receive equalization payments from the federal government.

have province

a province whose per capita tax revenue exceeds a certain average level and which does not therefore receive equalization payments from the federal government.

stabilization payment

a payment made especially by the federal government to a region or sector in order to stabilize a faltering economy.

transfer payment

a direct payment from a government not made in exchange for goods or services, e.g. to an individual or family in the form of an employment insurance payment or family allowance, or (in Canada) especially to another level of government.

upload

shift (costs) from a lower level of government to higher one.

Who's Who

Auditor General

the official responsible for auditing the accounts of a (federal or provincial) government's agencies, departments, and some Crown corporations, and presenting an annual report on government spending to the House of Commons or legislature.

critic

a member of an opposition party monitoring and criticizing a specific government ministry.

Crown

the federal or provincial government.

GG

Governor General.

MHA

(in Newfoundland and Labrador) Member of the House of Assembly.

MLA

(in many provinces and the territories) Member of the Legislative Assembly.

MNA

(in Quebec) Member of the National Assembly.

MPP

(in Ontario) Member of Provincial Parliament.

superminister

a cabinet minister with responsibility for an important portfolio or a number of related portfolios.

Dropping the Writ: Elections (in) Canada

acclaim

elect without opposition.

acclamation

the act or an instance of election by virtue of being the sole candidate.

advance poll

an early poll for voters who expect to be absent from their riding on election day.

all-candidates meeting

a public meeting held during an election campaign at which all the candidates for an electoral district present their platforms and answer questions from the audience.

bagman

a political fundraiser.

borough

1 *historical* (in Ontario) a municipality with the status of a township. **2** (in Quebec) one of the municipal electoral divisions of the amalgamated city of Montreal.

chief electoral officer

an official appointed to oversee the conduct of federal, provincial, and territorial elections.

enumerate

1 enter (a person's name) on a list of voters for an election. **2** prepare the voters list for (an area), usually by conducting a house-to-house survey. **3** conduct such a survey.

enumerator

a person employed to conduct a survey to register voters for a voters list.

leadership convention

a convention held by a political party for the purpose of electing a new leader.

leadership race

a campaign of several candidates for the leadership of a political party.

mainstreeting

political campaigning in main streets to win electoral support.
❏ **Origin**: perhaps coined by John Diefenbaker in 1959.

poll captain

a person responsible for directing an election campaign for a candidate in a given area.

re-offer

(*Maritimes*) stand as a candidate for re-election.

riding

a district whose voters elect a representative member to a legislative body; a constituency or electoral district.

riding association

a unit of organization of a political party at the level of the riding, responsible for nominating a candidate for election and conducting the election campaign in the riding.

drop the writ

call an election.

Before the Courts

article
(of a law student) serve one's period of apprenticeship.

assize
1 a session of a court. **2** a trial or lawsuit held before a travelling judge.

bâtonnier
(in Quebec) the president of the Bar Association. ❑ **Pronunciation**: "bat on YAY". **Origin**: French, literally "staff bearer", from *bâton* "staff".

bencher
a member of the regulating body of the law society in all provinces except New Brunswick.

bijuralism
the existence of two legal systems within a single jurisdiction.

colour of right
the right of ownership of a thing.

Criminal Code
a Canadian federal statute embodying most of Canada's criminal law and specifying criminal procedures and sentencing options.

Crown attorney / Crown prosecutor / Crown counsel / Crown

a lawyer who conducts prosecutions of indictable offences on behalf of the Crown.

Crown witness

a witness called to testify by the Crown.

examination for discovery

a pretrial meeting to disclose the evidence that will be presented at a civil trial.

FAC

Firearms Acquisition Certificate.

factum

a statement of the facts of a case and the legal arguments which will be made, filed by each party in an appeal.

judicare

a form of legal aid in which lawyers bill the province for services to poor clients rather than receiving a salary.

junior

a young or new lawyer in a law firm.

Madam(e) Justice

a title given to a female appeal court judge.

notary

(*Quebec*) a member of the legal profession not authorized to plead in court but qualified to draft deeds, contracts, and other legal documents, e.g. wills, real estate transactions, etc.

principal

a lawyer who supervises an articling student.

Public Trustee

a provincial government official who administers the estates of people who die intestate, missing persons, etc.

show-cause hearing

a judicial hearing where a party involved in litigation must show cause why something must be done or must not be done, especially a hearing at which the prosecution shows cause why an accused should be kept in custody rather than granted bail.

sole practitioner

a lawyer, accountant, or other professional who is the sole member of a firm, rather than one who works in partnership with others.

student-at-law

an articling student.

On the Wrong Side of the Law

appearance notice

a written form given by a police officer to a person accused of a crime at the scene of the crime, stating the date, time, and place that the accused must appear in court.

criminal harassment

the criminal offence of stalking.

criminal negligence

an offence involving a wanton or reckless disregard for the lives or safety of others.

dangerous offender

a person who has been convicted of a serious personal injury offence and constitutes a threat to the life, safety, or physical or mental well-being of others, and whose history suggests little hope of reform, who is imprisoned indefinitely.

hybrid offence

a crime which may be treated as either a summary conviction offence or an indictable offence, at the discretion of the Crown.

impaired

(of driving or the driver of a car, boat, snowmobile, etc.) adversely affected by alcohol or narcotics, specifically for legal purposes, having a blood alcohol level greater than .08.

indictable offence

a more serious criminal offence, such as murder, which is triable by way of indictment.

public mischief

the criminal offence of making a false accusation, reporting an offence that did not occur, doing something that will cause another person to be suspected of an offence, etc.

restricted weapon

a firearm, especially a handgun, of a category that is strictly licensed and may be used only by licensed operators under specific conditions.

snitch line
a telephone number which a person can call anonymously in order to report another's non-compliance with particular laws, regulations, etc.

summary (conviction) offence
a relatively minor criminal offence tried by a magistrate and without a jury or preliminary hearing.

To Serve and Protect

Charter
(of a police officer) inform a person upon arrest of their rights under the Canadian Charter of Rights and Freedoms, particularly of the reason for the arrest and the right to a lawyer.

checkstop
(*Alberta*) a roadside checkpoint where drivers are randomly tested with a Breathalyzer.

CSIS
Canadian Security Intelligence Service. ❑ **Pronunciation**: "SEE sis".

detachment
the office or headquarters of a police district, especially one patrolled by the RCMP, OPP, etc.

ghost car
informal an unmarked police car.

horseman
slang a member of the Royal Canadian Mounted Police.

morality squad

a police unit dealing with infractions of legislation concerning prostitution, pornography, drugs, gambling, etc.

Mountie

informal a member of the RCMP.

North West Mounted Police

historical a federal police force established in 1873, renamed the Royal North West Mounted Police in 1904 and the Royal Canadian Mounted Police in 1920.

provincial police

(in Ontario and Quebec) a police force under provincial authority responsible for jurisdictions without municipal police protection.

RCMP

1 the Royal Canadian Mounted Police, Canada's national police force, which enforces federal statutes and provides policing for jurisdictions without municipal police protection in all provinces and territories except Ontario and Quebec. **2** *informal* an RCMP officer.

redcoat

historical a member of the North West Mounted Police.

RIDE

(*Ontario*) a program to reduce impaired driving, in which police stop vehicles randomly and check drivers for signs of intoxication, especially during the holiday season. ❑ **Origin**: acronym from "Reduce Impaired Driving Everywhere"

Sûreté (du Québec)

the provincial police force of Quebec. ❑ **Pronunciation**: "soor a TAY". **Origin**: French, = "police force", literally "safety".

In the Clink (or Not)

conditional sentence

a criminal sentence of up to two years that is served in the community rather than in jail under various conditions imposed by the trial judge, such as house arrest, curfews, community service, etc., the breaching of which may lead to incarceration.

day release

release of a jailed offender during the day or for a short period of time, e.g. to attend school or for employment.

gate

retain (an inmate, especially a dangerous offender) in prison for the full length of a sentence, by arresting the inmate as soon as he or she is released under mandatory supervision.

mandatory supervision

supervision by a parole officer of a convict serving the last part of a sentence in the community after being released from prison, usually because of good behaviour in the first two-thirds of the sentence.

open custody

custody in a correctional facility that has relatively little supervision or security, e.g. a group home etc.

secure custody / closed custody

custody in a correctional facility designed and designated for the detention of young offenders.

statutory release

parole as required by statute, especially after two-thirds of a sentence has been served.

LOONIE TUNES

Money

🍁 *Fun CanSpeak Facts:* Running out of Loonies 🍁

Business

Employment

Running out of Loonies

Imagine for a moment that you are a newcomer to Canada. Vending machines proclaim that they are for "loonies only" (the *Globe and Mail* used to have boxes that said "Loonies only on Saturdays"). Newspaper headlines say things like "Loonies to help crime victims" (an article about a fundraising drive) or "Loonie poised to make jump" (an article about the strengthening Canadian dollar). Or, recently arrived across the border from Detroit, you might see this sign at a Windsor Burger King, as I once did: "We are running out of loonies. If you have any, please provide them." Why does your northern neighbour want more insane people (and why are they helping crime victims)?

You would be equally flummoxed if, finding yourself in a store, you were accosted by a Canadian inquiring "Where's the cash?". But no, this is not a stickup, just an innocent question about the location of the cash registers.

There are many kinds of money that are unique to Canada, starting with the "funny money" of the Aberhart Social Credit party in 1937, ($25 certificates issued by the government to Albertans), which have an echo in the so-called Ralphbucks (officially "prosperity cheques") of $400 paid to every Albertan in 2006.

And then there's the currency that's sure to be found in a drawer somewhere in almost every Canadian household: Canadian Tire money.

As soon as you're dealing with real money, though, whether you're collecting pogey (or "stamps" as they say in Atlantic Canada) or working, even at a "joe-job", someone is definitely going to ask you "What's your SIN?" Your sin? What business is it of theirs?

SINs and loonies: everything you need to know about money in the True North.

It Makes the World Go Round

baby bonus
    family allowance or child tax benefit.

Bay Street / The Street
    1 a street in Toronto where the headquarters of many financial institutions are located. **2** the moneyed interests of Toronto, especially as opposed to other regions of Canada.

Canada Savings Bond / CSB
    a savings bond issued by the Canadian federal government.

Canadian Tire money
    coupons having the appearance of play money issued in varying small denominations to customers by associate stores of the Canadian Tire Corp. Ltd. for redemption on purchases.

certified general accountant
    a person trained and licensed to practise accounting.

funny money
    informal historical twenty-five-dollar certificates issued to Albertans in 1937 by the Social Credit government of Premier William Aberhart.

Heritage Fund

a fund established by a province, region, city, etc. from supplementary revenue either as a hedge against difficult economic times or as a resource for future social and cultural development.

Howe Street

1 a street in Vancouver where the offices of many financial institutions are located. **2** the moneyed interests of Vancouver, especially as opposed to other regions of Canada.

loonie

1 the Canadian one-dollar coin. **2** *informal* the Canadian dollar.

Maple Leaf

a one-ounce gold coin, bearing the image of a maple leaf, produced by the Royal Canadian Mint.

Ralphbucks

slang a $400 cheque issued to every Albertan in 2006 out of a large government budget surplus. ❏ **Origin**: after Ralph Klein, then premier of Alberta.

RESP

Registered Educational Savings Plan, a tax-sheltered plan for saving money for a child's post-secondary education.

St. James Street

1 a street in Montreal where the offices of many financial institutions are located. **2** the moneyed interests of Montreal, especially as opposed to other regions of Canada.

shinplaster

historical slang a banknote worth twenty-five cents. ❏ **Origin**: from its resemblance to a square piece of paper soaked in vinegar and used as a bandage for the shin, known as a shinplaster.

toonie

informal the Canadian two-dollar coin.

Taxes

GST

goods and services tax, a value-added tax levied on a broad range of consumer goods and services. (Also used in New Zealand.)

HST

harmonized sales tax, a value-added tax on goods and services combining the GST and the provincial sales tax in Nova Scotia, New Brunswick, and Newfoundland and Labrador.

PST

provincial sales tax.

QST

Quebec Sales Tax.

RevCan

slang Revenue Canada (the former name of the Canada Revenue Agency).

user-pay

designating a program the costs of which are paid for by user fees.

welcome tax

(*Quebec*) a municipal tax levied on all house purchases in the Province of Quebec. ❏ **Origin**: translation of French *taxe de bienvenue*.

Pensions

CPP

Canada Pension Plan, a pension plan funded by contributions from employees and employers and administered by the Canadian government.

GIS

Guaranteed Income Supplement, a federally-supported supplement to the monthly pension payments of those with little income other than that derived from Old Age Security.

LIF

life income fund, a tax-sheltered fund providing annual income to its holder, not falling below an established minimum percentage of the fund, but also not exceeding a maximum payment.

LIRA

locked-in retirement account, a retirement savings account created with money transferred out of a registered pension plan and from which funds can only be transferred to a life income fund, a locked-in retirement income fund, or a life annuity.

LRIF

locked-in retirement income fund, a tax-sheltered savings plan which provides retirement income.

OAP

Old Age Pension.

OAS

old age security, a system of government-funded pensions for those over 65.

QPP

Quebec Pension Plan.

RRSP

Registered Retirement Savings Plan, a tax-sheltered plan for saving for retirement.

Spouse's Allowance

a federal benefit paid to low-income 60–64-year-old spouses of Old Age Security pensioners.

Banking

ABM

automated banking machine.

bank machine

an electronic machine which allows users to perform banking transactions by inserting an encoded plastic card.

bank rate

the central bank's minimum interest rate on short-term loans to banks etc.

the Big Six

the six leading Canadian banks.

caisse populaire

    (in Quebec and other francophone communities) a co-operative financial institution similar to a credit union.

chartered bank

    a large, privately-owned bank chartered by Parliament and operating under the provisions of the Bank Act.

GIC

    guaranteed investment certificate, a certificate guaranteeing a fixed interest rate on a sum of money deposited with a financial institution for a fixed term, usually between one and seven years, which may not be withdrawn before term.

Instant Teller

    proprietary a bank machine.

Interac

    proprietary a system of payment by means of a debit card, in which funds are transferred electronically from the cardholder's bank account to the account of a merchant etc.

near bank

    a financial institution, e.g. a credit union or caisse populaire, that provides banking services but does not have the status or privileges of a chartered bank.

term deposit

    an amount of money, usually between $1,000 and $5,000, deposited with a financial institution for a fixed term, usually between 30 days and a year, at a fixed interest rate, and which can be withdrawn before term on payment of a penalty.

Mortgages

closed

(of a mortgage etc.) that may not be paid off before the stated term without a financial penalty.

convertible

designating a mortgage which may not be paid off before the stated term without a financial penalty, but which may be converted to a longer term without penalty.

open

(of a mortgage etc.) that may be paid off in full without penalty before the expiry of the stated term.

BUSINESS

bonusing

an act of subsidizing something, especially as an inducement for development etc.

branch plant

a factory etc. owned by a company based in another country.

cash

informal a cash register.

corporate welfare bum

slang derogatory **1** a business perceived to be exploiting tax loopholes, capital gains concessions, etc. or to be benefiting unduly from government subsidies or tax breaks. **2** a person who directs such a business. ❏ **Origin**: coined by David Lewis, federal NDP leader 1971–75.

Crown corporation

a corporation owned by the federal or provincial governments, e.g. Canadian Broadcasting Corporation, Canada Post, etc.

moose pasture

slang a piece of land promoted as having mining potential but in fact unproductive.

numbered company

a corporation the name of which is simply its registration number followed by the province in which it is registered.

tollgate

a barrier imposed illegally on business or trade etc. pending payment of a bribe or tribute.

tollgating

the illegal practice of paying or extorting a bribe or tribute for the right to do business with or within a province, country, etc.

EMPLOYMENT

---

book off

stay home from work, especially when sick.

employment equity

a hiring policy encouraging fair representation of women, visible minorities, native people, handicapped people, etc. in the work force.

employment insurance / EI

a federal government program providing payments to eligible unemployed people, funded by tax revenues and contributions by employers and workers. Formerly called unemployment insurance.

help-wanted index

a rough, seasonally adjusted measure of the job market calculated from help-wanted advertisements in newspapers.

insurable earnings

income on which employment insurance premiums are paid.

isolation pay

a financial supplement to the salary of an employee who works in an isolated area, usually in the Far North.

joe job

a menial or monotonous task.

lieu time

time taken off work in compensation for overtime worked.

make-work

designating a project, program, grant, etc. intended to create jobs, especially one sponsored by the government.

pogey / pogy

informal **1** unemployment insurance benefits. **2** welfare benefits.

Rand formula

a stipulation in most union agreements that all employees within a bargaining unit must pay union dues, but that actual membership in the union is voluntary. ❑ **Origin**: I.C. Rand, Canadian judge, arbitrator, and educator, d.1969.

social insurance number / SIN

a nine-digit number by which the federal government identifies individuals for the purposes of taxation, employment insurance, pensions, etc.

stamps

(*Atlantic Canada*) **1** *historical* adhesive pieces of paper affixed by an employer to an employee's record of employment, collected by the employee to prove eligibility for employment insurance. **2** *slang* employment insurance benefits.

summer student

a student, especially a university student, working at a job for the summer.

T4 (slip)

an official statement issued by an employer, indicating one's employment income for the year, as well as the amount paid in employment insurance premiums and contributions to the Canada Pension Plan etc., used to calculate the amount of taxes owed and submitted with one's tax return.

UIC

1 *historical* Unemployment Insurance Commission. **2** *informal* unemployment insurance.

unemployment

informal unemployment insurance, the former name for employment insurance.

vacation pay

the wages which an employee is entitled, under federal law, to receive either as paid vacation, or in lieu of paid vacation, amounting to four per cent of the year's salary or six per cent for an employee who has worked for a single employer for six or more consecutive years.

CRADLE
TO
GRAVE

Health and Medicine
🍁 *Fun CanSpeak Facts:* Putting the Care in Medicare 🍁

Schools and Education

Social Services

Garbage and Recycling

Putting the care in medicare

Imagine you are a new arrival in Canada and you have unfortunately sprained your ankle. "Are you going to emerg?" a helpful Canadian might ask. "Emerge? Emerge from where?" would be your instant reaction. If you are in Kingston or Windsor or St. Catharines, once you get past that misunderstanding, you might be even more confused to find that the hospital you arrive at is called the "Hotel-Dieu". The "hotel of God", what a bizarre name for a hospital, you think. Anywhere in Canada, if you are American, you will notice that many Canadians, like the British, go "to hospital" and stay "in hospital", without the article "the". At emerg (a handy name for the emergency department not only at hospitals across Canada but even at veterinary emergency clinics), you would probably be advised to tape your ankle with a Tensor bandage, a brand name used generically that is unknown in the US, where elasticized bandages are known by another trade name, "Ace" bandages.

Indeed, trade names that we take for granted for items at our drugstore could cause us problems when we're travelling. Say we come down with motion sickness; our first Canadian instinct is to go to the drugstore for some Gravol (it doesn't matter if it's the actual Gravol brand or the generic dimenhydrinate pills; who ever asks for dimenhydrinate in Canada?). If you were to ask for Gravol in an American or British drugstore, they would think, perplexedly, that you are asking for gravel. The trade name they use is Dramamine.

If you have a headache, Aspirin is, fortunately, a word that is recognized throughout the English-speaking world. In fact, outside of Canada, it has lost its trade name status altogether. But in Canada, only Bayer has the legal right to call its tablets of acetylsalicylic acid "Aspirin". As a result, Canadians have another name for the substance, ASA (the full form being a bit of a mouthful!). Although most Canadians are unlikely to ask for an "ASA" when they have a headache, they are at least familiar with the abbreviation, unlike other speakers of English.

Canadians consider our health care system as a cornerstone of our identity; it is not surprising, therefore, that we have our own words for many things relating to it.

ASA

acetylsalicylic acid, the active ingredient in Aspirin.

blood donor clinic

a usually temporary location where people can give blood.

CLSC

(in Quebec) a provincially funded community health care clinic. ❏ **Origin**: abbreviation of *centre local des services communautaires*, literally "local community services centre".

denticare

a plan for providing dental care funded by some provincial governments.

emerg

slang a section of a hospital for handling emergencies.

extra-billing
the practice of a doctor charging patients fees in excess of what provincial health insurance will pay.

Gravol
proprietary dimenhydrinate, a medication used to counter nausea and vomiting and prevent motion sickness.

hallway medicine
the practice of treating hospital patients on beds in hallways because of a shortage of hospital rooms.

health card
a card identifying a person as eligible to receive medical treatment paid for by a public insurance plan.

Hotel-Dieu
a name given to a hospital in French-speaking areas or to one established by a French-speaking order of nuns.

medicare
a national health care program financed by taxation and administered by the provinces and territories.

nursing station
a clinic or small hospital in a remote community, staffed by nurses and visited regularly by a doctor.

OHIP
Ontario Health Insurance Plan.

pharmacare
(in some provinces) a system of subsidization of drug costs, especially by the government.

redirect

a situation in a hospital emergency department where ambulances with all but critically ill patients are redirected to another hospital.

Tensor bandage

proprietary a wide elasticized bandage used to tape injured joints to provide support.

Victorian Order of Nurses

a non-profit community-based health organization that provides home care for the elderly and chronically ill.

VON

1 the Victorian Order of Nurses. **2** a VON nurse.

SCHOOLS AND EDUCATION

Types of Schools

CEGEP

(in Quebec) Collège d'enseignement général et professionnel, a post-secondary educational institution offering two-year programs for preparation for university and three-year training programs in professions and trades. ❑ **Pronunciation**: "SEE jep" or "SAY zhep".

collège classique / classical college

historical (in Quebec) a private school offering a four-year secondary education and a four-year post-secondary program leading to a BA, with the curriculum emphasizing classics, literature, philosophy, and religion.

collegiate and vocational institute

(in Ontario) a public secondary school, originally one having academic, vocational, and commercial streams.

collegiate (institute)

(in some provinces) a public secondary school, originally one having specialist teachers and a prescribed classical curriculum.

composite (high) school

(in Alberta) a secondary school offering both vocational and academic courses.

comprehensive high school

a secondary school offering both vocational and academic courses.

consolidated school

a school replacing several smaller schools in a district.

integrated school

(*Newfoundland*) *historical* a public school established, maintained, and operated jointly by members of the Anglican, United, and Presbyterian Churches and the Salvation Army.

junior college

(*Quebec*) *informal* a CEGEP.

public school

(*Ontario*) **1** a school that is part of the public school system.
2 an elementary school that is part of the public school system.
3 elementary schooling in the public school system.

public school system
> a system of publicly-funded non-denominational schools, as distinct from the publicly-funded separate (Catholic) schools.

regional school
> a school located centrally within a region, usually a rural one, taking the place of several smaller schools.

separate school
> **1** (in Ontario) a publicly funded school for Catholic students. **2** (in Alberta and Saskatchewan) a publicly funded school for children belonging to the religious minority (usually Catholics) in a given district.

Hitting the Books

bird course
> *derogatory slang* a university or high school course requiring little work or intellectual ability.

browner
> (*Ontario*) *informal* a person who behaves obsequiously in the hope of advancement; a brown-noser.

bursary
> a financial award to a student, especially a university student, made primarily on the basis of financial need or some other criterion in addition to academic merit.

calendar
> a list of courses offered at a university or college, along with general information on registration etc.

CanLit

informal Canadian literature.

CanStud

Canadian studies

co-instructional

(*Ontario*) extracurricular; not included in the normal curriculum.

co-op

informal an educational program in which students alternate terms in the classroom with terms in the workforce in a job related to their studies.

don

a senior person in a university residence, usually responsible for the students and community life.

intersession

a short university term, usually in May and June, in which the course material usually covered in thirteen weeks is condensed into five or six weeks of intensive study.

junior kindergarten / JK

(*Ontario*) a class for young children, usually ages 3 to 4, which prepares them for kindergarten through games, singing, socialization, etc.

keener

informal a person, especially a student, who is extremely eager, zealous, or enthusiastic.

niner

(especially *Ontario*) *slang* a student in grade nine, the first year of high school.

res

slang a university or college residence.

semestering

an educational system in which the school year is divided into two terms having school days with a reduced number of longer periods, with the whole year's course material in any given subject concentrated into one or the other term.

senior kindergarten / SK

(*Ontario*) a class for young children, usually five-year-olds, in preparation for grade one.

spare

a period in one's school day schedule in which one is not required to be in class.

School's Out!

jig

(*Maritimes*) play truant from school.

March break

a school holiday, usually about a week long, in March.

professional development day / PD day

a day on which classes are cancelled so that teachers may attend seminars etc. for professional development.

reading week

a week usually halfway through a university term during which there are no classes, intended for students to concentrate on their reading, research, etc.

skip off

(*Southern Ontario*) play truant from school.

skip out

(*West*) play truant from school.

School Supplies

Duo-Tang

proprietary a report folder of light coloured cardboard, with three flexible metal fasteners to insert through the holes of loose-leaf paper.

pencil crayon

a pencil with a coloured core used for art, colouring, etc.

scribbler

a small, soft-covered booklet for writing in; a student's notebook.

What the Adults Do

home and school (association)

a local organization of parents and teachers to promote better communication and improve educational facilities.

supporter

a person who pays education taxes to a specified (public or separate) school system.

trustee

an elected member of a school board.

SOCIAL SERVICES

Children's Aid (Society) / CAS

an organization sanctioned to provide assistance or guardianship for homeless or abused children.

(native) friendship centre

an institution established in a predominantly non-Aboriginal community to provide counselling and social services etc. to Aboriginal people.

Imperial Order Daughters of the Empire / IODE

a Canadian women's organization founded in 1900 to promote British institutions in Canada, but more recently focusing on community affairs and supporting educational, cultural, and social causes in Canada.

interval house

a women's shelter.

Kinette

a member of a women's organization associated with the Kinsmen.

Kinsman

a member of a fraternal organization for especially businessmen and professionals, founded in 1920.

marriage commissioner

(in some provinces) an official who conducts civil marriages.

Public Curator

(*Quebec*) a provincial government official responsible for the affairs of persons legally unfit to conduct them themselves, e.g. a minor, a mentally incompetent person, etc.

transition house / transition home

a home operated by a social service agency, especially for abused women.

Women's Institute / WI

an organization founded to enable women in rural areas to meet regularly and engage in various cultural activities, social work, etc. Now worldwide, it was first established by Adelaide Hoodless in Stoney Creek, Ontario, in 1897.

GARBAGE & RECYCLING

blue box

a blue plastic box for the collection of recyclable household materials. ❏ **Origin**: first used in Kitchener in 1982.

garburator

a system installed in a kitchen sink, with blades in the drain to mulch refuse; a garbage disposal unit.

green bin

a green plastic bin used for curbside collection of recyclable or compostable materials, especially one for organic waste.

nuisance grounds

(*West*) a garbage dump.

redemption centre

(*Atlantic Canada*) a place where consumers return beer bottles, pop cans, etc. and receive back the deposit paid at the time of purchase.

swamper

(*BC*) an assistant to a truck driver, especially a garbage truck driver.

CANSTUD 101

Fun CanSpeak Facts:
🍁 Loyalists to Loonies: A Very Short History of Canadian English 🍁

Fur Trade

New France

Who Says Our History's Dull?

Loyalists to Loonies: A Very Short History of Canadian English

Many Canadians have but one, fearful, question about their language: is it becoming more American? In light of Canadian history, this is quite ironic, since the roots of Canadian English (other than Newfoundland English, which derives from the dialects of southwest England and of Ireland) are in the speech of the United Empire Loyalists who fled the United States during and after the Revolution. At its origins, then, Canadian English *was* American English, so it is hard to know how it could become *more* American. This common origin explains why Canadians share so many words with Americans and sound more like Americans from the northern states than they sound like the British. Much of the vocabulary that distinguishes North American English from British English is an inheritance of older words that have survived over here but been superseded by other words in the UK (fall for autumn, diaper for nappy, etc.). Likewise, we retain some older pronunciations (herb with a silent h, for instance, which can be traced back to the Middle Ages). But Canadian English is different from American English, and our history accounts for that.

Ever since our arrival in Canada, English speakers have co-existed with French speakers and aboriginal peoples. We have happily borrowed many words from both, a process that continues to this day. From early fur-trade borrowings such as "voyageur", to 19th-century borrowings like "tuque" to our most recent acquisitions like "poutine", Canadian English includes a lot of French! Words like "saskatoon" reveal our indebtedness to native languages.

In the 19th century, vast numbers of people from the British Isles were encouraged to settle in British North America to ward off any lurking nefarious American influence. Although their children inevitably ended up sounding like their playmates rather than their parents, some British linguistic traits managed to impose themselves. It is to this time that we owe our "British spellings", our use of "zed" rather than "zee", and the pronunciations that some (but not all) of us use (leftenant, shedule, herb with an h). Scots in particular left their mark on Canadian English. In the Maritimes, Southwestern Ontario, and the Prairies, people use Scottish words like "storm-stayed" and "a skiff of snow", but other Scottish words have made it into English across the country: "bursary" for a particular type of scholarship, "bannock" for a kind of quick bread (this usage probably thanks to the high numbers of "Orkneymen" in the employ of the Hudson's Bay Company).

Another phenomenon of the 19th century was the hybrid language used on the west coast known as "Chinook Jargon". This mixture of several aboriginal languages, particularly Nuu-chah-nulth and Chinook, with English and French, facilitated communication between the various groups. It was widely used but has now died out, though remnants of it survive in such words as "chum (salmon)", "Siwash sweater", and "saltchuck".

The 20th century brought waves of immigrants from non-English speaking countries, as we saw with our look at Ukrainian and Italian words in Canadian English. As we borrow from other languages, we continue to invent new words ("stagette") from and apply new senses ("download") to the existing English vocabulary.

Canadians may be consumed by the fear of being swallowed up entirely by US English, but we have already managed to maintain our linguistic distinctiveness despite living right next door to this behemoth for almost 250 years, with citizens travelling back and forth freely between both countries, and with Canadians bombarded constantly by a barrage of American publishing and media, the like of which other English-speaking countries never experience. I believe that Canadian English will continue to survive and thrive. Just so long, of course, as we don't run out of loonies.

FUR TRADE

country-born

designating English-speaking Protestants of mixed European and Aboriginal ancestry.

country marriage

a common-law marriage between a fur trader of European descent and an Aboriginal or Metis woman.

country wife

the Indian or Metis common-law wife of a fur trader.

coureur de bois

a French or Metis fur trader, especially one employed by the Hudson's Bay or North West Companies. ❑ **Origin**: French, = "runner of the woods".

factor

an employee of the Hudson's Bay Company, ranking higher than a chief trader, in charge of a trading post.

factory

a main trading post, especially a large centre for the transshipment of furs.

fur brigade

a convoy of Red River carts, York boats, canoes, etc. which transported furs and other commodities to and from isolated trading posts.

grease trail

any of the forest paths connecting the Pacific coast with the interior, used for centuries as trade routes. ❑ **Origin**: named by European settlers after eulachon oil, one of the most important commodities traded.

made beaver

a unit of exchange formerly used among fur traders, equivalent to the value of the prepared skin of one adult beaver in prime condition.

voyageur

a usually French-speaking or Metis canoeman employed by merchants in Montreal to transport goods to and from trading posts in the interior.

NEW FRANCE

filles du roi

women of marriageable age sent from France to New France under royal direction between 1663–73 to be married to the disproportionately large number of men then living in the colony. ❑ **Origin**: French, literally "daughters of the king".

habitant

a French settler in rural Quebec up until the early 20th century, especially a farmer. ❑ **Origin**: French "inhabitant".

seigneur

a holder of land under the seigneurial system.

seigneurial system

a system of land tenure established in New France, based on the feudal system, under which land was owned by seigneurs who rented it to tenant farmers and provided mills, a court system, and other services. The system was left in place after the Conquest, and was officially abolished in 1854.

seigneury

1 a tract of land held by a seigneur under the seigneurial system. **2** a grant of land in the interior, especially for the harvesting of furs, fish, etc.

WHO SAYS OUR HISTORY'S DULL?

Barr Colonists

a group of about 2000 English colonists, led originally by the Rev. Isaac Barr, who settled the area west of Saskatoon from 1903 onward.

Blue Puttees

the first 500 volunteers to join the Royal Newfoundland Regiment at the outbreak of war in 1914.

Origin: so-called because there was not enough of the standard khaki material available for the soldiers' puttees and blue cloth was used instead.

Château Clique

a name given to the small group of powerful citizens appointed to important political positions by the governor in Lower

Canada prior to 1830. Mostly English-speaking merchants, they tended to promote their own interests instead of addressing the problems of the French-speaking majority.

Clergy Reserves

Crown lands set aside during the settlement of Upper and Lower Canada, the revenue from which was to be used to support Protestant clergy. They caused considerable political debate until the land was secularized in 1854.

The Conquest

the British conquest of French North America in 1763.

Crow rate

a reduced rate for shipping grain or flour by rail from Western Canada to Eastern Canada. ❑ **Origin**: legislated by the Crow's Nest Pass Agreement in 1897, ensuring a subsidy to the Canadian Pacific Railway in return for the reduced rate.

dirty thirties

informal **1** the Great Depression of the 1930s. **2** the years of drought coinciding with this on the Prairies, accompanied by vast dust storms.

Family Compact

1 a name given to the ruling class in Upper Canada in the early 19th century, especially to the members of the legislative and executive councils. This governing Tory elite was held together by ties of family, patronage, and social and political beliefs, and promoted British institutions such as a social hierarchy and an established Church. **2** any influential clique or faction.

Father of Confederation

any of the delegates who represented colonies of British North America at the Charlottetown and Quebec Conferences or the London Conference, which led to Confederation in 1867.

home child

one of a number of orphaned or destitute children sent from Britain to Canada from the mid-19th to the early 20th century to serve as farm or domestic help.

late Loyalist

an American settler who came to Canada between 1790 and 1800 after the influx of the first United Empire Loyalists.

Lower Canada Rebellion

an armed uprising against British rule in Lower Canada beginning in the late fall of 1837, when rising tensions between French nationalists (led by Louis-Joseph Papineau) and the pro-British governing party prompted the government to attempt to arrest the leading French-Canadian reformers, who fled to the countryside. Regular troops pursued, and the subsequent battles which put down the rebellion left more than 300 dead.

Mackenzie-Papineau Battalion / Mac-Paps

a Canadian military formation of approximately 1300 volunteers which fought in the International Brigades against the Nationalist forces of General Franco during the Spanish Civil War. ❏ **Origin**: Named for William Lyon Mackenzie and Louis-Joseph Papineau, leaders of the Rebellions of 1837.

(United Empire) Loyalist / UEL

1 any of the colonists of the American revolutionary period who supported the British cause, many of whom afterwards migrated to Canada. **2** a descendant of such a person.

Maple Leaf

the Canadian flag.

Medicine Line

(*West*) the Canada–US border, especially from Ontario westward.

October Crisis

the kidnapping of the British diplomat James Cross and the Quebec labour and immigration minister Pierre Laporte by separate cells of the Front de Libération du Québec in October of 1970, resulting in the federal government's invoking of the War Measures Act to allow for the detention of some 450 suspected FLQ members; Laporte was murdered by his kidnappers, who were arrested and convicted; Cross was released in exchange for the safe passage of his captors to Cuba.

Patriote

a supporter of Louis-Joseph Papineau in the 1837 Rebellion of Lower Canada.

postage stamp province

a nickname for Manitoba from 1870 to 1881, during which time the province's boundaries resulted in it looking like a small square postage stamp.

Quiet Revolution

in Quebec, the period under the Liberal provincial government of Jean Lesage from 1960 to 1966, characterized by province-wide social, economic, and educational reforms, as well as mounting separatist sentiment and the issue of a special status for Quebec within Confederation.

Selkirk settler

an early settler at the Red River Settlement (Manitoba) founded by the Earl of Selkirk in 1812.

Trail of '98

the route taken by stampeders during the Klondike gold rush of 1898, including the Chilkoot Pass.

Upper Canada Rebellion

an armed uprising against British rule in Upper Canada beginning in the late fall of 1837, in which reformers and radicals led by William Lyon Mackenzie attempted to seize control of the government in Toronto. The rebels were badly disorganized, however, and were easily dispersed in two main skirmishes, one near Toronto and another a few days later near Brantford.

whisky fort / whisky post

an establishment selling whisky illegally to the Aboriginal peoples of the Canadian west in the late 19th century.

zombie

slang (during World War II) a conscript, originally for national defence as opposed to overseas service.

THE BRITISH CONNECTION

❧ *Fun CanSpeak Facts:* Rule Britannia ❧

Rule Britannia

Canadians often state categorically to me that Canadian English is closer to British English than to American English. They fervently believe this, in spite of the numerous differences of accent and vocabulary (do "court" and "caught" sound the same for us? do we put nappies on our babies and buy packets of crisps?) between Canadian and British English.

What they are thinking of, of course, is spelling.

One day at my local supermarket I had the enlightening experience of witnessing a linguistic debate carried out on the sign over the plants and potting soil. The unfortunate who had written the sign called his department a "Garden Center". Some zealot had come along with a black felt marker, crossed this out and replaced it with "Centre", accompanied by the adjuration "Spell Canadian!". The horticultural manager stood his ground, however, and wrote a note to the effect that this *was* Canadian spelling. It is true that on the whole, British spellings are more common in Canada, but there are some notable exceptions. We buy automotive supplies at the "Canadian Tire" (not "tyre") store and park our cars at the "curb" (not "kerb"). All the same, if a Canadian talks about "Canadian spelling", you can be sure that they are talking about spelling "colour" with an -our ending.

One thing that unites almost all Canadians is the desire to show the world that we are most emphatically NOT AMERICANS! And what could be a simpler, more effective way to do this than to write colour with a *u* and traveller with two *l*'s? That'll show those Yankees!!

Because we believe this so fervently, some of us get our shirts in a knot (if we really spoke British English we would instead get our knickers in a twist) about how to spell words like "organize". Some Canadians mistakenly believe that the *-ise* spelling for this suffix is the "Canadian" spelling because they are aware that Americans use only the *-ize* variant and that the British prefer the *-ise* variant. However, this British preference is only recent, and *-ize* has always been the preference of Oxford University Press and until recently *The Times* of London, with the justification being that this suffix is ultimately derived from a Greek and Latin spelling in which *z* rather than *s* is used. The vast majority of Canadians who do use the *-ize* spellings are therefore not traitors to Canadian identity. They are following, not American practice, but former British practice and long-standing Canadian practice.

It is time for Canadians to assert that we use not British or US spelling but something we could call Canadian spelling, without looking over our shoulders to either imperial power. This is a blend of both spelling conventions, with the odd (or perhaps I should say occasional!) uniquely Canadian variant such as "yogourt". This, it would seem, arose as a result of bilingual labelling laws. The spelling yogourt has the advantage of working both in Canadian English and Canadian French (where the word is preferred over the continental French *yaourt*), and thus the yogourt manufacturers have to print it only once on the tubs of their product. Another uniquely Canadian spelling phenomenon is that we are more likely to use the American spelling "plow" for literal uses ("the streets hadn't been plowed yet") but the British "plough" for figurative uses ("I've got a ton of papers to plough through").

Apart from spelling, however, there are indeed some words that Canadians share with the British (and often other Commonwealth countries) but not with Americans. They make up a much smaller part of our vocabulary than the words we share with Americans. Over 5000 words in the *Canadian Oxford Dictionary* are labelled "North American", compared to fewer than 500 words labelled "Canadian and British". Predictably, parliamentary institutions and the law (including policing) account for many of these. But others we use every day, and it is quite surprising to learn that Americans don't. Most of us know that Americans don't call the last letter of the alphabet "zed", but do they really never say "bum" to mean "buttocks"? How can little Yankees make it through childhood without playing king of the castle, or getting the bumps on their birthdays? Here is a small selection of words that Canadians share with British English speakers.

anaesthetist

a medical doctor specializing in the administration of anaesthetics.

annual general meeting / AGM

a yearly meeting of members or shareholders, especially for holding elections and reporting on the year's events.

Bob's your uncle

informal an expression of completion or satisfaction.

browned off

informal fed up, disheartened.

bum

informal the buttocks.

the bumps

a custom in which a person celebrating a birthday is either lifted by the legs and arms and lowered to the ground or hit in the buttocks with a knee once for each year of age.

by-election

an election held in a single constituency to fill a vacancy arising during a government's term of office.

bylaw

a law made by a body subordinate to a legislature, especially a municipal government.

candy floss

a fluffy mass of spun sugar wrapped around a stick.

cheese strings

cheese, usually mozzarella or cheddar, that has been pulled into strands which are pressed or braided together into a cylinder but may be pulled off to be eaten individually.

claw back

1 regain laboriously or gradually. **2** recover (money paid out) from another source (e.g. by taxation).

codswallop

informal nonsense.

(police) constable

a police officer of the lowest rank.

detached

(especially of a house) separate, not joined to another or others.

digestive cookie / digestive biscuit

a usually round semi-sweet whole wheat cookie.

dozy
   informal slow-witted or lazy.

exercise book
   a book for writing school work, notes, etc., in.

ginormous
   informal very large; enormous.

gynie
   informal **1** a gynecologist. **2** gynecology.

half-cut
   informal fairly drunk.

hard done by
   harshly or unfairly treated.

humbug
   a hard candy usually flavoured with peppermint.

icing sugar
   finely powdered sugar, usually combined with a small amount
   of cornstarch, for making icing for cakes etc.

J-Cloth
   proprietary a type of light, absorbent, reusable cloth used for
   household cleaning.

kerfuffle / kafuffle
   informal a fuss or commotion.

king of the castle

a children's game consisting of trying to displace a rival from an elevated position.

Limited

(after a company name) designating a company whose owners are legally responsible only to a limited amount for its debts.

market garden

a place where vegetables and fruit are grown for the market etc.

marketing board

an association of agricultural producers controlling the marketing of a specific commodity, often setting prices and imposing production quotas.

mat leave

informal maternity leave.

physio / physiotherapy

the treatment of disease, injury, deformity, etc., by physical methods including manipulation, massage, infrared heat treatment, remedial exercise, etc., rather than by drugs.

piss down

slang rain heavily.

railway

a railroad.

rejig

reconfigure, rearrange; reorganize.

return ticket

a ticket for a journey to a place and back to the point of origin.

running on the spot

raising the feet alternately as in running but without moving forwards or backwards.

Sally Ann

informal the Salvation Army.

semi(-detached)

a house joined to another by a shared wall on one side only.

serviette

a napkin for use at table, especially a paper one.

Snakes and Ladders

a game in which counters are moved by dice throws along a board on which snakes and ladders are depicted, a counter that lands on the head of a snake being moved back to the tail, while one that lands at the foot of a ladder advances to the top.

soother

a ring or nipple made of rubber or plastic given to a baby to suck.

staff room

1 a common room for staff, especially in a school.

supply teacher

a substitute teacher.

tea towel

a thin linen or cotton towel for drying washed dishes etc.

zed

the letter Z.

What do you call people from . . . ?

Abbotsford: Abbotsfordians
Airdrie: Airdrites
Ajax: Ajacians
Alberta: Albertans
Amherst: Amherstonians
Antigonish: Antigonishers
Arnprior: Arnpriorites
Arviat: Arviaqmiut
Aurora: Aurorans
Baddeck: Baddeckers
Banff: Banffites
Bathurst: Bathurstonians
Bedford: Bedfordites
Belleville: Bellevillians
Brandon: Brandonites
British Columbia: British Columbians
Brockville: Brockvillians
Burlington: Burlingtonians
Calgary: Calgarians
Campbell River: Campbell Riverites
Campbellton: Campbelltonians
Camrose: Camrosians
Canmore: Canmorites
Cape Breton: Cape Bretoners / Capers
Charlottetown: Charlottetonians
Chatham: Chathamites
Cobourg: Cobourgers

Cochrane: Cochranites
Coquitlam: Coquitlamites
Corner Brook: Corner Brookers
Cranbrook: Cranbrookers
Crowsnest Pass: Crowsnesters
Dartmouth: Dartmouthians
Dauphin: Dauphinites
Dawson: Dawsonites
Delta: Deltans
Devon: Devonians
Digby: Digbyites
Duncan: Duncanites
Eastern Townships: Townshippers
Edmonton: Edmontonians
Edson: Edsonites
Elliot Lake: Elliot Lakers
Espanola: Espanolians
Estevan: Estevanites
Fernie: Fernieites
Fort Erie: Fort Erians
Fort Frances: Fort Francians
Fort Smith: Fort Smithers
Fredericton: Frederictonians
Gananoque: Gananoqueans
Gander: Ganderites
Gaspé: Gaspesians
Georgina: Georginians
Goderich: Goderichites
Grand Manan Island: Grand Mananers
Grande Prairie: Grande Prairians
Guelph: Guelphites
Haileybury: Haileyburians
Halifax: Haligonians

Hamilton: Hamiltonians
Hanover: Hanoverians
Harbour Grace: Harbour Gracians
Hawkesbury: Hawkesburians
Hay River: Hay Riverites
High River: High Riverites
Hinton: Hintonites
Hudson: Hudsonites
Humboldt: Humboldtonians
Huntsville: Huntsvillians
Îles de la Madeleine: Madelinots
Iqaluit: Iqalungmiut
Jasper: Jasperites
Kamloops: Kamloopsians
Kenora: Kenorans
Kentville: Kentvillites
Kincardine: Kincardinites
Kingston: Kingstonians
Kitimat: Kitimatians
Labrador: Labradorians
Lacombe: Lacombians
Leamington: Leamingtonians
Leduc: Leducians
Lincoln: Lincolnites
London: Londoners
Lunenburg: Lunenburgers
Madawaska: Madawaskans
Magdalen Islands: Madelinots
Mahone Bay: Mahone Bayers
Manitoba: Manitobans
Manitoulin Island: Haweaters
Maritimes: Maritimers
Meaford: Meafordites

Medicine Hat: Hatters
Melville: Melvillites
Milton: Miltonians
Miramichi: Miramichiers
Mission: Missionites
Mississauga: Mississaugans
Moncton: Monctonians
Montreal: Montrealers
Moose Jaw: Moose Javians
Morden: Mordenites
Nanaimo: Nanaimoites
Neepawa: Neepawans
Nelson: Nelsonites
New Brunswick: New Brunswickers
New Westminster: New Westminsterites
Newfoundland: Newfoundlanders / Newfies (*informal*) /
    Newfs (*informal*)
Niagara Falls: Niagarans
North Bay: North Bayites
Nova Scotia: Nova Scotians / Bluenosers (*informal*) /
    Bluenoses (*informal*)
Nunavut: Nunavummiut
Oak Bay: Oak Bayers
Oakville: Oakvillians
Ontario: Ontarians
Orillia: Orillians
Oromocto: Oromoctonians
Ottawa: Ottawans
Otterburn Park: Otterburners
Parry Sound: Parry Sounders
Peace River: Peace Riverites
Pelham: Pelhamites
Pembroke: Pembrokians

Perth: Perthites
Petrolia: Petrolians
Pictou: Pictonians
Port Alberni: Port Albernians
Port Colborne: Port Colborners
Port Elgin: Port Elginites
Port Hope: Port Hopers
Portage la Prairie: Portagers
Powell River: Powell Riverites
Prince Albert: Prince Albertans
Prince Edward Island: Prince Edward Islanders / Islanders
Prince George: Prince Georgians
Prince Rupert: Rupertites
Quebec: Québécois / Quebecers
Quispamsis: Quispammers
Red Deer: Red Deerites
Red Lake: Red Lakers
Regina: Reginans
Revelstoke: Revelstokians
Richmond: Richmondites
Richmond Hill: Richmond Hillers
Sackville: Sackvillians
Saint John: Saint Johners
St. Stephen: St. Stepheners
Sarnia: Sarnians
Saskatchewan: Saskatchewanians
Saskatoon: Saskatonians
Sault Ste. Marie: Saultites
Selkirk: Selkirkians
Sherbrooke: Sherbrookers
Simcoe: Simconians
Sioux Lookout: Sioux Lookouters
Smithers: Smithereens

Spallumcheen: Spallumcheenites
Spruce Grove: Spruce Grovers
Steinbach: Steinbachers
Stettler: Stettlerites
Stoney Creek: Creekers
Stratford: Stratfordians
Sudbury: Sudburians
Surrey: Surreyites
Sydney: Sydneyites
Taber: Taberites
Terrace: Terracites
Thorold: Thoroldites
Tillsonburg: Tillsonburgers
Toronto: Torontonians / Hogtowners (informal)
Trail: Trailites
Trenton: Trentonians
Truro: Truronians
Twillingate: Twillingaters
Vancouver: Vancouverites
Victoria: Victorians
Walkerton: Walkertonians
Wallaceburg: Wallaceburgers
Wasaga Beach: Wasaga Beachers
Welland: Wellanders
Westmount: Westmounters
Whistler: Whistlerites
White Rock: White Rockers
Wiarton: Wiartonians
Williams Lake: Williams Lakers
Windsor: Windsorites
Winkler: Winklerites
Winnipeg: Winnipeggers
Woodstock: Woodstonians

Yarmouth: Yarmouthians
Yellowknife: Yellowknifers
Yukon Territory: Yukoners

APPENDIX 2

Test your knowledge of Canadian English!

1. What is an immigrant to Quebec who speaks neither English nor French called?
   a) allophone
   b) optophone
   c) autrophone
   d) aboiteau

2. What is the name used, especially in Ontario, for a farm building in which machinery (tractors, combines, etc.) is stored?
   a) equipment barn
   b) garage
   c) drive shed
   d) machine barn

3. In Newfoundland, a cossack is
   a) a derogatory name for a Western Canadian of Ukrainian descent
   b) a type of fishing boat
   c) a derogatory name for a foreign trawler that fishes within the 200-mile limit
   d) a type of parka

4. Which of the following sports is uniquely Canadian?
   a) floor hockey
   b) ice fishing
   c) five-pin bowling
   d) all of the above

5. What is a francophone who lives in Quebec called?
   a) a Québécois
   b) a Québecois
   c) a Quebécois
   d) none of the above

6. Which of the following derogatory names for a person (for example a student) who is just a little too eager to do his or her work is not used in the US?
   a) an apple polisher
   b) a keener
   c) a brown-noser
   d) all of the above

7. What is the hooded parka in which Inuit women carry their babies called?
   a) angakok
   b) amautik
   c) aglu
   d) alliak

8. In which city might you order a jambuster?
   a) Winnipeg
   b) Edmonton
   c) Guelph
   d) Halifax

9. Which region of Canada has a unique sense for the word "across"?
   a) Newfoundland
   b) Vancouver Island
   c) PEI
   d) Baffin Island

10. Which of the following is a uniquely Canadian word?
    a) arborite
    b) alderman
    c) agent general
    d) all of the above

11. What does a Newfoundlander mean by "airsome"?
    a) haughty, pretentious
    b) windy
    c) cold, invigorating
    d) silly, airheaded

12. What kind of trees would you find in an Acadian forest?
    a) amabilis fir, arbutus, redwood
    b) alpine fir, lodgepole pine, arborvitae
    c) balsam fir, red spruce, yellow birch
    d) Douglas fir, Alberta spruce, paper birch

13. Which of the following terms is uniquely Canadian?
    a) closed shop
    b) closed mortgage
    c) closed captioning
    d) closed circuit

14. Which of the following words is used on the West Coast to mean the ocean?
    a) chuck
    b) brinepond
    c) coldwash
    d) clearwater

15. Which of the following words and phrases is not used in the US?
    a) Bob's your uncle
    b) bargoon
    c) physiotherapy
    d) all of the above

16. The term Château style designates
    a) an autocratic form of government practised in New France
    b) a style of dress characterized by funky, youthful, trendy clothing
    c) a style of architecture best exemplified by the grand Canadian railway hotels of the early twentieth century
    d) a premium-quality wine of the Niagara peninsula

17. The word carspiel is a Canadianism meaning:
    a) the patter of a used-car salesman
    b) the incessant chatter kept up by children in the back seat of a car on long journeys
    c) a Canadian winter activity based on curling, played on large expanses of cleared lake ice, with the object being for one driver in a car to knock other cars out of a painted circle
    d) a curling competition at which the prize is a car

18. Which of the following etymologies has been suggested to explain why Nova Scotians are called Bluenoses?
    a) they are named after a variety of potato which has a long, thin, blueish protuberance
    b) it was originally a derogatory designation for highly puritanical Scottish Presbyterians, and was applied by

Loyalists to Nova Scotians, many of whom were Scottish Presbyterians.

c) many Nova Scotians are fishermen, and acquire blue noses from being out in the cold so much.

d) all of the above

19. By what other name do Montrealers know bobskates?
    a) cheesecutters
    b) catamarans
    c) bi-blades
    d) babiches

20. Which Canadian Prime Minister first used the word "main-streeting" to mean political campaigning?
    a) Pierre Elliott Trudeau
    b) John A. Macdonald
    c) Arthur Meighen
    d) John Diefenbaker

21. Which charitable social organization originated in Canada?
    a) Women's Institute
    b) Victorian Order of Nurses
    c) Kinsmen
    d) all of the above

22. What is the name of Canada's spoof political party?
    a) Hippopotamus Party
    b) Albertosaurus Party
    c) Rhinoceros Party
    d) Gopher Party

23. A Calgary red-eye is
    a) an overnight Calgary-Halifax flight
    b) a tourist who has stayed up all night partying at the Stampede
    c) a drink of beer and tomato juice
    d) a form of conjunctivitis that is common amongst workers on oil rigs

24. Muskox wool is
    a) qiviut
    b) qallunaat
    c) qajaq
    d) qulliq

25. Which of the following words for school supplies is unique to Canada?
    a) pencil crayon
    b) Duo-Tang
    c) scribbler
    d) all of the above

26. Which is not a level of amateur sports?
    a) mosquito
    b) bantam
    c) blackfly
    d) atom

27. A slang name for a piece of land promoted as having mining potential which is in fact worthless is
    a) muskox tundra
    b) moose pasture
    c) caribou ground
    d) elk meadow

28. A slang name for a beer belly is
    a) Labatt muscle
    b) Sleeman's muscle
    c) Kokanee muscle
    d) Molson muscle

29. Which of the following is not a uniquely Canadian dessert:
    a) butter tart
    b) mangia-cake
    c) matrimonial cake
    d) Nanaimo bar

30. Sludgy masses of densely packed sea ice are
    a) slob ice
    b) bum ice
    c) hangashore ice
    d) messy ice

31. The revenge of the cradle is
    a) the tendency of babies to wake up at 4 in the morning
    b) an extremely high birthrate amongst French Canadians in the nineteenth century
    c) retaliation by a much younger lover dumped by an older person
    d) the cost of raising a family

32. A steamie in Quebec is
    a) a hot humid day
    b) a hot dog
    c) a pornographic movie
    d) a sauna

33. The Newfoundland cake made from rice, pork, and molasses is
    a) lumpgut
    b) bangbelly
    c) thudpot
    d) heavytummy

34. A hamburger only found in Canada is the
    a) Louisbourger
    b) iceberger
    c) Amherstburger
    d) banquet burger

35. Which canoe was once paddled along Canadian water-ways?
    a) jackass canoe
    b) bastard canoe
    c) scuzzball canoe
    d) doofus canoe

36. A young harp seal is a
    a) chaoser
    b) hurlyburlier
    c) bedlamer
    d) uproarer

37. In Saskatchewan a hooded sweatshirt is a
    a) bunny hug
    b) kangaroo cuddle
    c) gopher snuggle
    d) prairiedog squeeze

38. A western wedding wouldn't be complete without which dance?
   a) grasshopper
   b) cricket
   c) butterfly
   d) blackfly

39. A popular Canadian drink:
   a) empress
   b) caesar
   c) seigneur
   d) czar

40. A Newfoundland drink of spruce beer, rum and molasses:
   a) callisham
   b) calliphony
   c) callibogus
   d) callifake

41. If you visit Atlantic Canada but are not from there, you're a
   a) don't-belong-here
   b) come-from-away
   c) come-in-on-the-tide
   d) wash-up-on-the-shore

42. A clump of trees on the prairies:
   a) bluff
   b) fake
   c) ruse
   d) deke

43. A Digby chicken is a
    a) chicken
    b) seagull
    c) clam
    d) herring

44. Newfoundland twilight is
    a) duckish
    b) gullish
    c) ternish
    d) chickenish

45. The kinder, gentler f-word:
    a) fumble-on
    b) fuddle-duddle
    c) fussy-fit
    d) funnel-cloud

46. A New Brunswicker is a herring _____
    a) kisser
    b) catcher
    c) choker
    d) eater

47. The Canadian term "Texas gate" refers to something designed
    to bar the passage of
    a) coyotes
    b) rats
    c) cattle
    d) illegal immigrants

48. From what type of fruit did Saskatoon get its name?
    a) a berry
    b) an apple
    c) a plum
    d) a coconut

49. You're likely to be a Canadian if you use which of these baseball terms?
    a) dugout
    b) backcatcher
    c) baserunner
    d) bullpen

50. A sign you'll see only in Canada:
    a) Garden Centre
    b) Auto Centre
    c) Tire Centre
    d) Medical Centre

ANSWERS:

				50. c)	49. b)
48. a)	47. c)	46. c)	45. b)	44. a)	43. d)
42. a)	41. b)	40. c)	39. b)	38. c)	37. a)
36. c)	35. b)	34. d)	33. b)	32. b)	31. b)
30. a)	29. b)	28. d)	27. b)	26. c)	25. d)
24. a)	23. c)	22. c)	21. d)	20. d)	19. a)
18. d)	17. d)	16. c)	15. d)	14. a)	13. b)
12. c)	11. c)	10. a)	9. c)	8. a)	7. b)
6. b)	5. a)	4. c)	3. d)	2. c)	1. a)

WORD INDEX